RENTAL MATERIALS

An orchestration consisting of **Piano/Conductor Score** and the **Vocal Chorus Books** will be loaned two months prior to the production ONLY on the receipt of the Licensing Fee quoted for all performances and the rental fee.

Please contact Baker's Plays for perusal of the music materials as well as a performance license application.

CHARACTERS

HAVERSHAM – A young housemaid, an ex-convict
RITA – A social secretary
MISS MAPLE – A well-known society hostess
FATHER WHITE – A mystery writer
CHANDLER MARLOWE – Another
LOUIS CROISSANT – Another
RICK – Another
LAURA – Another
PETER FLIMSEY – Another
CHARITY – Another
SERVANTS – Chorus (Optional)

NOTES ON THE CHARACTERS

In the program be sure to list the fictitious roles of Mabel Dupre and Pharoah Link. This way the audience assumes two "new" characters are always about to appear and shed some light on the mystery.

It is suggested the names be added between Charity and the Servants, MABEL DUPRE - A mysterious woman, and PHAROAH LINK - A detective. The names of two fictitious actors are needed, as well.

PLACE

Ravenswood Manor, an isolated estate on Turkey Island, off the coast of San Francisco.

TIME

The Present.

SETTING

Act One

Scene 1: The sitting room. Afternoon.

Scene 2: *The sitting room. Later.*

Act Two

Scene 1: *Still later.*

Scene 2: *Early morning.*

The Butler Did It, Singing

A Musical Spoof in Two Acts
Based on the Play *The Butler Did It*

Book by Tim Kelly
Music by Arne Christiansen
Lyrics by Ole Kittleson

Baker's Plays
7611 Sunset Blvd.
Los Angeles, CA 90042
BAKERSPLAYS.COM

NOTICE

This book is offered for sale at the price quoted only on the understanding that, if any additional copies of the whole or any part are necessary for its production, such additional copies will be purchased. The attention of all purchasers is directed to the following: this work is fully protected under the copyright laws of the United States of America, the British Commonwealth, including Canada, and all other countries of the Copyright Union. Violations of the Copyright Law are punishable by fine or imprisonment, or both. The copying or duplication of this work or any part of this work, by hand or by any process, is an infringement of the copyright and will be vigorously prosecuted.

This play may not be produced by amateurs or professionals for public or private performance without first submitting application for performing rights. Licensing fees are due on all performances whether for charity or gain, or whether admission is charged or not. Since performance of this play without the payment of the licensing fee renders anybody participating liable to severe penalties imposed by the law, anybody acting in this play should be sure, before doing so, that the licensing fee has been paid. Professional rights, reading rights, radio broadcasting, television and all mechanical rights, etc. are strictly reserved. Application for performing rights should be made directly to BAKER'S PLAYS.

No one shall commit or authorize any act or omission by which the copyright of, or the right to copyright, this play may be impaired. No one shall make any changes in this play for the purpose of production.

Publication of this play does not imply availability for performance. Both amateurs and professionals considering a production are strongly advised in their own interest to apply to Baker's Plays for written permission before starting rehearsals, advertising, or booking a theatre.

Whenever the play is produced, the author's name must be carried in all publicity, advertising and programs. Also, the following notice must appear on all printed programs, "Produced by special arrangement with Baker's Plays."

Licensing fees for THE BUTLER DID IT, SINGING is based on a per performance rate and payable one week in advance of the production.

Please consult the Baker's Plays website at www.bakersplays.com or our current print catalogue for up to date licensing fee information.

Book Copyright © 1986 by Tim Kelly, 2010 by the Estate of Tim Kelly
Lyrics Copyright © 1986, 2010 by Ole Kittleson
Made in U.S.A.
All rights reserved.

THE BUTLER DID IT, SINGING
ISBN 978-0-87440-377-0
#4164-B

MUSICAL NUMBERS

OVERTURE

ACT ONE

MURDER, MYSTERY, MAYHEM . . . . Miss Maple, Haversham, Rita, (Staff)

SUCH A WITTY COUPLE . . . . .Rick, Laura, Guests

WHAT'S HER GAME . . . . Detectives

MURDER IS MY BUSINESS . . . . .Chandler

THE MOTH TO THE FLAME . . . . .Father White, Laura

THE BUTLER DID IT. . . . . Entire Cast

ENTR'ACTE

ACT TWO

I KNOW MY STUFF. . . . . .Charity

CHERCHEZ LA FEMME. Peter, Male Detectives

I AM LOUIS CROISSANT . . . . Louis

REVELATIONS . . . . .Company

FEMME FATALE . . . . .Mabel

Reprise: THE BUTLER DID IT . . . . Entire Cast

ACT I

Scene One

*(**SETTING:** The sitting room of Ravenswood Manor, on Turkey Island, off the coast of San Francisco. It's a shadowy enclave with a brooding quality "made for mystery." Downstage right there's an exit or servant's door leading to other rooms, including the kitchen. Upstage center is a small hallway that leads offstage for the second story. Stage left are doors, possibly French doors, that open onto an unseen balcony. Depending on the individual stage size, the set is generous with Gothic lamps, bric-a-brac, carpets, furniture. However, the essential pieces are as follows: a fireplace with mantel stage right, with a large portrait hanging above. The subject is a dour, but impressive-looking gentleman. On the mantel there are three figurines. Upstage right there is a console. Upstage left a bookcase. Downstage left there is a desk, chair, and wastebasket. There is a sofa downstage right center and a small table and comfortable chair left center. Prior to curtain, sound of a motorboat approaching the island.)*

*(**AT RISE:** **HAVERSHAM**, a slovenly maid, is standing at the French doors, one of which is open. She stares off. **HAVERSHAM** is a mousey creature cursed with a case of the sniffles. Her uniform hangs on her body as if it were two sizes too big. She wears large glasses.)*

HAVERSHAM. *(rubs her arms, talks out to audience)* Brrrrr. Another day for foul weather. I can feel it in my big toe. The one on my left foot. It's better than a barometer. *(calls upstage)* I can see the motorboat docking, Miss Maple.

(HAVERSHAM *looks off again. Sound of motorboat cutting engine.* MISS MAPLE *enters upstage center, a commanding dowager with a lively sense of adventure.*)

MISS MAPLE. I love mystery weekends.

HAVERSHAM. *(sniffles)* Do you think all your guests will show up?

MISS MAPLE. I guarantee it. *(as she moves to sofa, sits)* What's the matter with your uniform?

HAVERSHAM. How do you mean, ma'am?

MISS MAPLE. Looks large enough for half-a-dozen people.

HAVERSHAM. Yes, ma'am.

MISS MAPLE. Can't you take it in?

HAVERSHAM. Won't do no good. No matter what I put on it'll look like a potato sack. I'm hard to fit.

MISS MAPLE. If you don't sniffle perhaps no one will notice the uniform.

HAVERSHAM. *(sniffles as she curtsies)* Yes, ma'am. Whatever you think best.

(RITA EYELESBARROW *enters downstage right carrying a large hatbox.*)

RITA. Everything's ready, Miss Maple.

MISS MAPLE. *(into audience)* Ah, my faithful social secretary and overpaid companion. *(to* RITA*)* I see you have your hatbox with you, Rita.

(RITA *hugs the hatbox tightly, fiercely – as if she feared* MISS MAPLE *might leap and snatch it away.*)

HAVERSHAM. If you ask me it ain't normal the way she hangs on to that hatbox. It's like she's got something in it she don't want no one to see.

(*There's no love lost between* RITA *and* HAVERSHAM.)

RITA. *(snarls)* No one's asking you for your opinion, droopy dress.

(HAVERSHAM *bares her teeth, snaps a few times.*)

How dare you!

MISS MAPLE. Ladies, please. Your manners.

HAVERSHAM. *(curtsies)* Yes, ma'am.

MISS MAPLE. *(shift in mood)* I can't seem to find the guest list

RITA. *(crosses)* On the desk, Miss Maple. *(picks up paper)*

MISS MAPLE. The logical place. That's why I didn't think of it

(**RITA** *crosses back to sofa, hands* **MISS MAPLE** *the paper.*)

HAVERSHAM. Beg pardon, Miss Maple. I'm not sure I understand about this mystery weekend.

RITA. You're not paid to understand.

(**HAVERSHAM** *bares her teeth.*)

MISS MAPLE. That will be enough of that.

HAVERSHAM. *(curtsies)* Yes, ma'am.

MISS MAPLE. I'II explain it again.

HAVERSHAM. Yes, ma'am. Thank you, ma'am.

MISS MAPLE. Don't slobber, Haversham. Your sniffles are bad enough.

HAVERSHAM. Didn't mean to slobber. I only want to please.

MISS MAPLE. Then pay attention. *(taps paper)* Each guest, none of whom I've met in person, is a famous mystery writer.

HAVERSHAM. *(repeats softly in mumbled fashion)* Famous mystery writer...

MISS MAPLE. Each guest will spend the weekend here at Ravenswood Manor as his alter-ego.

HAVERSHAM. Alter what?

MISS MAPLE. *(irritated by* **HAVERSHAM***'s lack of understanding)* My guests will appear as the detective hero or heroine of their books.

HAVERSHAM. *(out to audience)* Whatever that means. *(to* **MISS MAPLE***)* Is it legal?

MISS MAPLE. Better than legal – exciting and thrilling.

HAVERSHAM. *(unimpressed)* Yes, ma'am. If you say so.

MISS MAPLE. *(the list)* What an array of personalities.

HAVERSHAM. What's an "array"?

MISS MAPLE. A veritable smorgasbord.

HAVERSHAM. What's a smorgasbord?

MISS MAPLE. *(again the list)* We have Louis Croissant

HAVERSHAM. *(mumbles)* Louis Croissant…

MISS MAPLE. The famous French detective. Extremely eccentric, but deft. Father White-

HAVERSHAM. *(mumbles)* Father White…

MISS MAPLE. He uses the psychological approach. Freudian mumbo-jumbo.

HAVERSHAM. *(mumbles)* Mumbo-jumbo…

MISS MAPLE. Peter Flimsey – he's in the Sherlock Holmes school.

HAVERSHAM. He's a student?

MISS MAPLE. Of life, Haversham. Of life. That's what makes a superior detective. *(delighted with the weekend's prospects)* I have a feeling my guests are going to get more than they suspect.

RITA. How do you mean, Miss Maple?

*(**MISS MAPLE** jumps to her feet, sings.)*

SONG – MURDER, MYSTERY, MAYHEM

MISS MAPLE.

(verse)
THIS WEEKEND JUST COULDN'T BE BRIGHTER.
THE GUEST LIST WAS CAREFULLY PLANNED.
YOU'LL FIND EV'RY MYSTERY WRITER
HAS A STYLE THAT'S UNUSUALLY GRAND.

THERE MAY BE SOME MYST'RY
THERE MAY BE SOME MAYHEM
WITH A MURDER TUCKED-IN BETWEEN.
SO THE MASTER-PLANNER
OF RAVENSWOOD MANOR
MAY HAVE SOME "REMAINS TO BE SEEN!"

(NOTE: The **CHORUS** *that appears from time to time is strictly optional. The* **CHORUS***, if utilized, represents "staff" at Ravenswood Manor. It can be any number — 2, 4, 6. A cook, a gardener, a chauffeur, a housekeeper. CAUTION:* **There is no butler.** *If you're doing a "small-scale" production simply omit* **CHORUS***.)*

(As **MISS MAPLE** *sings,* **STAFF** *enters left and right.)*

HAVERSHAM, RITA & (STAFF).

(echo)
BE SEEN!

MISS MAPLE.

(first chorus)
MURDER MYSTERY, MAYHEM.
KILLING,
FOUL-PLAY,
SLAYING,
SUFFOCATION.
HANGING,
DROWNING,
STABBING,
STRANGULATION.
SOMEONE MAY KICK THE BUCKET.
WE'LL WIND UP SEARCHING FOR CLUES.
AND WITH A LITTLE LUCK IT'LL BE
A WEEKEND THAT'S BOUND TO AMUSE.

(second chorus)
MURDER, MYSTERY, MAYHEM.
PUZZLES,
SECRETS,
RIDDLES,
MISCONCEPTIONS.
SHADY
DEALINGS,
BLACKMAIL,
GROSS DECEPTIONS.
WATCH OUT FOR RIGOR MORTIS.
HE MAY WANT TO SPEND THE NIGHT.
AND WITH A LITTLE LUCK IT'LL BE
A WEEKEND THAT'S BOUND TO DELIGHT.

MISS MAPLE. *(cont.)*
 (third chorus)
 MURDER, MYSTERY, MAYHEM.
 HAZARDS,
 PERILS,
 MALICE,
 THREATS AND DANGERS.
 MENACE,
 DOUBLE
 CROSSES,
 EVIL STRANGERS.
 SKELETONS IN THE CLOSET
 JUST LIKE "AND THEN THERE WERE NONE"
 AND WITH A LITTLE LUCK IT'LL BE
 A WEEKEND THAT'S JOLLY-GOOD FUN.

HAVERSHAM & RITA.
 MURDER, MYSTERY, MAYHEM.

HAVERSHAM.
 KILLING.

RITA.
 FOUL-PLAY,

HAVERSHAM.
 SLAYING,

RITA.
 SUFFOCATION.

HAVERSHAM.
 HANGING,

RITA.
 DROWNING,

HAVERSHAM.
 STABBING,

RITA.
 STRANGULATION

MISS MAPLE.
 SOMEONE MAY KICK THE BUCKET.
 WE'LL WIND UP SEARCHING FOR CLUES.

ALL.

AND WITH A LITTLE LUCK IT'LL BE
A WEEKEND THAT'S BOUND TO AMUSE.

HAVERSHAM & RITA.

MURDER, MYSTERY, MAYHEM.

RITA.

PUZZLES,

HAVERSHAM.

SECRETS,

RITA.

RIDDLES,

HAVERSHAM.

MISCONCEPTIONS.

RITA.

SHADY

HAVERSHAM.

DEALINGS,

RITA.

BLACKMAIL,

HAVERSHAM.

GROSS DECEPTIONS.

MISS MAPLE.

WATCH OUT FOR RIGOR MORTIS.
HE MAY WANT TO SPEND THE NIGHT.

ALL.

AND WITH A LITTLE LUCK IT'LL BE
A WEEKEND THAT'S BOUND TO DELIGHT.

ALL.

MURDER, MYSTERY, MAYHEM.
HAZARDS,
PERILS,
MALICE,
THREATS AND DANGERS.
MENACE,
DOUBLE
CROSSES,
EVIL STRANGERS.

MISS MAPLE.
> SKELETONS IN THE CLOSET
> JUST LIKE "AND THEN THERE WERE NONE"

ALL.
> AND WITH A LITTLE LUCK IT'LL BE
> A WEEKEND THAT'S JOLLY-GOOD FUN.
>
> *(tag)*
> THE WEEKEND WILL BE EXCITING
> EV'RYTHING A-NUMBER-ONE.
> SO, HERE'S TO "HOME, SWEET HOMICIDE!"
> WITH MURDER, MYST'RY, MAYHEM AND FUN!
>
> *(As song ends,* **STAFF** *exits.)*

MISS MAPLE. Run down to the beach and guide them up, Haversham.

HAVERSHAM. *(curtsies, sniffles)* Yes, ma'am. *(exits left)*

RITA. Do you think Haversham is suitable, Miss Maple?

MISS MAPLE. I promised the parole people I would be patient with her.

RITA. *(surprised)* You mean she's an ex-convict?

MISS MAPLE. Haversham is on a work program. If she works out well her parole is assured. Much will depend on my report.

RITA. What was her crime?

MISS MAPLE. I believe it was something disagreeable she did with a hatchet.

RITA. *(moves left, stares outside)* A hatchet! I don't like the sound of that.

MISS MAPLE. Compose yourself, Rita. There'll be quite enough melodrama when my guests arrive. *(the list)* Chandler Marlowe – there's a man to reckon with. Seedy, down and out, but intelligent in a brutish sort of way. A true male chauvinist.

RITA. I wish I had known about Haversham before I took this job.

MISS MAPLE. I had second thoughts about Charity Haze. Too much like James Bond for my taste. *(pockets list)* All and all it'll be a delightful *menage.*

RITA. I hope you know what you're doing, Miss Maple. Here's your first guest.

MISS MAPLE. Bravo.

(FATHER WHITE *enters. He wears a clerical collar, carries a rolled umbrella. His manner is slightly doddering.*)

FATHER WHITE. (*to* RITA) Ah, Miss Maple. I'd know you anywhere. Delighted, delighted.

RITA. I'm not Miss Maple.

FATHER WHITE. Eh?

RITA. That's Miss Maple. (RITA *indicates* MISS MAPLE, *moves to bookcase.*)

FATHER WHITE. (*crossing*) Ah, Miss Maple. I'd know you anywhere. Delighted, delighted.

MISS MAPLE. You're Father White. (*They shake hands.*)

FATHER WHITE. Amazing. How did you know?

MISS MAPLE. You're wearing a clerical collar.

FATHER WHITE. Remember the first rule of detection, Miss Maple. *Disregard the obvious.* I might be Louis Croissant in disguise.

MISS MAPLE. (*enchanted*) Touché. (*nods to* RITA) My social secretary and companion, Miss Eyelesbarrow.

RITA. Welcome to Turkey Island.

FATHER WHITE. Too kind.

MISS MAPLE. (*indicates sofa*) Please be seated. Sherry and warm biscuits shortly.

FATHER WHITE. Splendid.

(*He sits.* CHANDLER MARLOWE, *a "tough private eye" type wearing a fedora, raincoat, enters. Hands in pockets. His voice is raw meat, talks from the side of his mouth.*)

MISS MAPLE. (*playfully*) I wonder who this could be? Hee, hee.

CHANDLER. (*turns profile*) Take a look at this distinctive nose, sister. These gray eyes. This jaw of stone.

MISS MAPLE. Chandler Marlowe.

CHANDLER. Better believe it, doll.

MISS MAPLE. *(indicates chair at desk)* Please be seated. Sherry and warm biscuits shortly.

CHANDLER. Sherry and warm biscuits?

(He makes a distasteful face at the thought, sticks a finger down his throat to let audience know he might vomit. Instead of the chair, he sits on the edge of desk. **LOUIS CROISSANT** *enters.)*

MISS MAPLE. Look, Rita. Unmistakably Louis Croissant.

LOUIS. You mustn't jump to transfusions, dear lady. I might be Charity Haze in drag.

*(***LOUIS*** *speaks with a French accent and frequently mispronounces English words. He wears a beret, a colorful ascot and neatly-trimmed moustache. In short,* **LOUIS** *is quite dapper. He notices the portrait over the fireplace, moves to it.)*

Ah, a most unusual painting. I must investigate. It appears to be an American style called paint-by-numbers.

(Laughter from off left followed by entrance of the debonair **RICK** *and* **LAURA CARLYLE**. **RICK** *carries a stuffed dog.)*

MISS MAPLE. I'd know you two anywhere. Mr. and Mrs. Carlyle.

FATHER WHITE. They brought along their little dog.

CHANDLER. Don't look now but that "little dog" is stuffed. I don't mean with Alpo.

RICK. We couldn't take our real bow-wow.

CHANDLER. How come?

LAURA. Gets seasick.

RICK. I said to Laura – "Who's going to know it's Rick and Laura without their pooch Napoleon?"

CHANDLER. Why'd'ya name your dog after a pastry?

LOUIS. *(moves down to others)* Ah, the Napoleon. It is a delicious pastry. French, you know. *(to* **LAURA***)* I see you have brought your little dog. Does he bite?

LAURA. No, he's stuffed.

LOUIS. Ah, a stuff-id dog. *(He pats the dog's head.)* Ah, good boy. Good Napoleon.

*(***LAURA*** *barks as if dog were alive.* ***LOUIS*** *recoils.)*

You told me he was a stuff-id dog. *(He shakes a finger at the dog.)* Naughty Napoleon. Bad dog. Don't come to me for a treat. *(to others)* Give a dog a mile and he'll take an inch.

*(***RICK*** *and* ***LAURA*** *bark and snarl at* ***LOUIS***. *All laugh except* ***LOUIS***.*)*

MISS MAPLE. *(to* **CHANDLER***)* Such a witty couple.

RICK & LAURA. How true.

*(***RICK*** *and* ***LAURA*** *move down center, sing.)*

SONG – SUCH A WITTY COUPLE

RICK & LAURA.

SUCH A WITTY COUPLE
BLASE AND STIMULATING
WE'RE DECIDEDLY CULTURED
AND SCINTILLATING.
OUR SENSE OF HUMOR HAS WHIMSICAL FLAIR
PROVOKING MIRTH WITH OUR DISTINCTIVE
    SAVOIR-FAIRE.

SUCH A WITTY COUPLE
THE GUESTS ARE ALL DELIGHTED
WHEN THEY PEEK AT THE GUEST LIST
AND SEE WE'RE INVITED.
FESTIVE AND SPARKLING AS BURGUNDY
THE DARLINGS OF SOCIETY.

WHEN WE DO OUR SLEUTHING
WE'RE INTOXICATINGLY GRAND
'CAUSE WE SOLVE EACH *MYST'RY*
AND COME TO OUR DEDUCTIONS
WITH A DRY MARTINI IN OUR HAND.

SUCH A WITTY COUPLE
AND SO SOPHISTICATED
WE'RE THE LIFE OF THE PARTY
IT CAN'T BE DEBATED.
AIRIER, MERRIER, WITH OUR FOX TERRIER
A WITTY COUPLE FULL OF FUN.

OTHERS.

(second chorus)
SUCH A WITTY COUPLE
BLASE AND STIMULATING
YOU'RE DECIDEDLY CULTURED
AND SCINTILLATING.

RICK & LAURA.

HAVING THE CARLYLES IS SIMPLY A MUST
ARISTOCRATIC LEADERS OF THE UPPER CRUST.

OTHERS.

SUCH A WITTY COUPLE
THE GUESTS ARE ALL DELIGHTED
WHEN WE PEEK AT THE GUEST LIST
AND SEE YOU'RE INVITED.

RICK & LAURA.

CHARMINGLY ELEGANT, WELL-TO-DO
WE'RE ALWAYS LISTED IN "WHO'S WHO!"
WHEN WE DO OUR SLEUTHING
WE'RE INTOXICATINGLY GRAND
'CAUSE WE SOLVE EACH MYST'RY
AND COME TO OUR DEDUCTIONS
WITH A SCOTCH-AND-SODA IN OUR HAND.

OTHERS.

SUCH A WITTY COUPLE
AND SO SOPHISTICATED
YOU'RE THE LIFE OF THE PARTY
IT CAN'T BE DEBATED.

RICK & LAURA.

MUST ADMIT
WE'RE A HIT
EV'RYONE'S FAVORITE
A WITTY COUPLE FULL OF FUN.

ALL.
> DEBONAIR
> WITH A FLAIR
> AND A RARE SAVOIR-FAIRE
> A WITTY COUPLE FULL OF FUN.
>
> *(As song finishes,* **PETER FLIMSEY** *enters, the very model of a proper English gentleman, A bit of a prig,* **LAURA** *sits beside* **FATHER WHITE. RICK** *sits left center.)*

PETER. Hi, ho, everyone.

MISS MAPLE. It's Pretty Flimsey.

PETER. It's *Peter.* Peter Flimsey.

MISS MAPLE. Welcome to Turkey Island.

PETER. *(steps into room)* I could hardly resist an invitation to visit Ravenswood Manor. The name conjures up pictures of the English moors – dark, brooding, mysterious.

MISS MAPLE. Oooooh. You talk the way you write.

> *(***PETER** *takes her hand, kisses it.)*

CHANDLER. Don't look sanitary to me, slobbering over a dame's knucklebones.

MISS MAPLE. Please be seated.

CHANDLER. Park it here, Flimsey.

> *(He pulls out the desk chair.* **PETER** *crosses, sits.)*

FATHER WHITE. Are we all accounted for?

RITA. We're missing Charity Haze.

MISS MAPLE. *(calls left, to outside)* Don't keep us waiting, Miss Haze.

> *(Pause.* **HAVERSHAM,** *sniffling, enters.)*

HAVERSHAM. I think I'm coming down with something.

RITA. We're not interested in you. Where is Miss Haze?

HAVERSHAM. How should I know?

FATHER WHITE. She wasn't with us on the boat.

LAURA. We assumed she arrived earlier.

MISS MAPLE. Go along, Haversham. Fetch refreshments. Try not to drop anything.

HAVERSHAM. I'll try.

(*She crosses downstage right, turns, curtsies. Exits sniffling.*)

LAURA. I wonder who does her dresses?

MISS MAPLE. I do hope you all like blue cheese fondue.

GUESTS. Blue cheese fondue?

(*They all make sour faces, turn aside and stick a finger into their mouth indicating they might upchuck.* MISS MAPLE *doesn't notice.*)

RITA. I'll see that everything's prepared upstairs.

(*She exits upstage center.* LOUIS *watches her go.*)

LOUIS. An interesting woman. Has she been with you long?

MISS MAPLE. A month.

PETER. Why do you ask?

LOUIS. When the moment is ripe, I shall harvest my deduction. At this point, however, I am not ready to jump out of the frying pan into the fireplace.

CHANDLER. We going to sit around and chew the fat?

RICK. It's either that or blue cheese fondue.

OTHER GUESTS. Let's chew the fat.

LAURA. I think there's going to be a storm. (*THUNDER*)

MISS MAPLE. (*claps her hands for attention*) Your attention, please. I will go over the ground rules and, then, we will proceed with our charade. You know of my reputation as an outstanding hostess with a fine imagination for all that is bizarre and unique. (*polite applause*) You've all done well so far. You look and act precisely like your creations. However – (*all tense*) I insist you keep up our "little game of pretend" at all times. Otherwise you may have to pay a forfeit. (*Laughs gaily. Others imitate her laugh.*)

I'll be watching…and listening. If the weekend turns out the way I trust it will, you will all receive wonderful news. News that will benefit you – *financially.*

GUESTS. Financially! (*All sit up, alert.*)

MISS MAPLE. I trust you are willing to play along?

AD LIBS. Yes. Of course. Sure. Why not? Sounds like fun. Wonderful idea.

CHANDLER. I'm with you, little sister. All the way.

MISS MAPLE. *(girlish laughter)* Chandler, you're a rare customer.

CHANDLER. I like to think of myself as well-done.

*(**MISS MAPLE** laughs. Again, the others laugh to humor her. Hostess exits downstage right. The instant she's off, the laughter ceases abruptly.)*

RICK. What's her game?

CHANDLER. Does it matter? You heard the old girl. If we do it her way we'll benefit. *Financially.*

LOUIS. Money, like sweet-smelling flowers, attracts the bumblebees.

CHANDLER. *(offended)* Are you calling me a bumblebee?

LOUIS. I am calling you nothing. I simply smell danger from the top of my head to the tips of my toenails.

LAURA. I get the feeling she's concealing something. If we're smart we'll play along and discover what she's up to. It could be fun. Agreed?

OTHERS. Agreed.

*(**LAURA** stands, sings.)*

SONG – WHAT'S HER GAME?

LAURA.

(verse)
OH, THIS WEEKEND WE'LL HAVE SUCH A GLORIOUS TIME
PLAYING GAMES GUESSING WHERE? WHY? AND WHO?

RICK.
WARM BISCUITS AND SHERRY ARE GOING TO BE SERVED.

CHANDLER.
ALONG WITH SOME BLUE CHEESE FONDUE.

FATHER WHITE.
DEAR, OLD RAVENSWOOD MANOR IS SUITABLY BLEAK
WITH A FLAVOR THAT THRILLS AND EXCITES.

PETER.

THE ATMOSPHERE'S GLOOMY,
THE FOG'S ROLLING IN.

ALL.

IT'S RIGHT OUT OF "WUTHERING HEIGHTS."

LOUIS.

AND OUR HOSTESS IS PECULIAR.
THATS A FACT YOU MUST ADMIT.
YES, MISS MAPLE'S AN ENIGMA.

ALL.

WE DON'T TRUST HER ONE BIT!

RICK.

WHATS HER GAME?
SHE IS CLEARLY UP TO SOMETHING
THOUGH I CAN'T DETERMINE JUST EXACTLY WHAT.

FATHER WHITE.

WHATS HER GAME?
IS SHE PLAYING BY THE RULE BOOK
WHILE HER MACHINATIONS THICKEN UP THE PLOT?

LAURA.

IT'S SO HARD
TO PREDICT HER CALCULATIONS
WITH RULES THAT NO ONE UNDERSTANDS.
BE ON GUARD
OF HER SLY MANIPULATIONS
OR WE MIGHT PLAY RIGHT INTO HER HANDS.

ALL.

WHAT'S OUR PLAN?
THE SOLUTION, WELL, OF COURSE, IS:
CALL HER BLUFF
STACK THE DECK WITH OUR RESOURCES
WE'LL TRUMP EV'RY ONE OF HER ACES
AND WIN THE GAME!

PETER.

WHAT'S HER GAME?
WELL, IT CLEARLY ISN'T CRICKET
AND I DON'T THINK IT'S A SIMPLE GAME OF CHESS.

LOUIS.

WHAT'S HER GAME?
IT IS NOT A GAME OF MAH JONGG
IT'S A GAME THAT TAKES THE ULTIMATE FINESSE.

CHANDLER.

THERE'S A GAME
WHERE YOU TRY TO LOAD THE BASES.
A GAME THAT TAKES A CERTAIN KNACK.
AND THIS DAME'S
GONNA TAKE US TO THE RACES.
YEAH, I THINK A JOKER'S IN THE PACK.

ALL.

WHATS OUR PLAN?
THE SOLUTION, WELL, OF COURSE IS:
CALL HER BLUFF
STACK THE DECK WITH OUR RESOURCES
WE'LL TRUMP EV'RY ONE OF HER ACES WITHOUT DELAY.
IT'S A GAME!
JUST LIKE POKER AND GIN.
IT'S A GAME!
THAT WE'RE GOING TO WIN!
IT'S A GAME AT WHICH TWO CAN PLAY!

(*SCREAM from downstage right.* **HAVERSHAM** *runs in.*)

HAVERSHAM. Miss Maple! Miss Maple! Miss Maple! (*In her excited state she immediately turns and exits.*)

CHANDLER. Is she advertising pancake syrup?

(**HAVERSHAM** *runs back in.*)

HAVERSHAM. (*frantic*) Miss Maple! Miss Maple! Miss Maple!

LAURA. (*a command*) Get a hold of yourself.

(*Which is precisely what* **HAVERSHAM** *does, wrapping her arms tightly around her body.*)

PETER. Why did you scream like that?

HAVERSHAM. It's the only way I know how to scream.

FATHER WHITE. What frightened you, child?

HAVERSHAM. I saw a face at the window. A horrible face Covered with hair.

RICK. Probably a stray dog. *(holds up a stuffed dog and jabs toward* **HAVERSHAM***)* Woof, woof.

HAVERSHAM. I don't think that's a bit funny. *(professional tone)* I'll see to the fondue. *(exits down right)*

CHANDLER. *(calls after her)* No hurry. *(to others)* Who's got the Turns?

RICK. I get the feeling I know Haversham's face.

LAURA. It's not a face you'd forget in a hurry. Especially in that dress. I never expected to attend one of Miss Maple's weekend parties. I've certainly read enough about them.

CHANDLER. There's more here than meets the private eye.

LOUIS. Not to mention the private eyebrow and eyelash.

CHANDLER. I hear the old lady's going to open a chain of bookstores.

OTHERS. Bookstores?

CHANDLER. Detective bookstores.

OTHERS. Detective bookstores!

CHANDLER. *(sly)* 'Course, none of you knew about that, did you?

(Others shake their heads innocently from side to side.)

We're all here for the same reason and it ain't to sample blue cheese fondue.

FATHER WHITE. Forget the fondue.

RICK. That won't be easy.

LAURA. *(to* **CHANDLER***)* You think we're all here to win Miss Maple's favor?

PETER. Thus insuring our detective novels a place on the shelves?

CHANDLER. That's the way I got it figured.

LAURA. Business is business and if Miss Maple wants to play games before placing an order with the publishers, I say – why not. If we don't play along she may not stock our books. That's the forfeit.

FATHER WHITE. *(to* **LAURA***)* I imagine you're glad about this. Your stuff is out of print as soon as it's published.

LAURA. If you weren't a man of the cloth, I'd have a few choice words for you.

CHANDLER. Mister French fries novels ain't doing much better, are they pal? *(to others)* Even the Nostalgia Book Club turned him down.

LOUIS. I read your last novel, Mr. Chandler, and found only two things wrong with it…the plot and the writing.

RICK. *(breaking in to avoid further conflict)*This is no way to start the weekend. We need to soften the mood. How about some light chamber music?

LAURA. Good idea. *(Moves to console. She snaps some dial. Radio blares immediately.)*

RADIO. We interrupt this program of light chamber music to bring you a special bulletin. *(All tense.)* A dangerous murderer has escaped from the Marin County Institute for the Criminally Insane. Known only as "The Killer of Forty Faces," the prisoner seized a rowboat at dawn and was last seen heading into a fog bank on the approach, to Turkey Island. Now, back to our program of light chamber music.

LAURA. *(snaps off radio)* Can it be true?

*(***MISS MAPLE*** enters downstage right.)*

MISS MAPLE. Sherry and biscuits.

*(***HAVERSHAM*** follows in with a tray of glasses and biscuits, which she sets down on some table.)*

FATHER WHITE. My congratulations, Miss Maple. A classic touch. The radio voice. I've used it several times in my own novels.

CHANDLER. Maybe that's why they don't sell.

MISS MAPLE. *(giggles)* I couldn't resist the radio voice. It's perfect for a mystery weekend.

("Guests" are anxious to please **MISS MAPLE** *and are overdoing their eagerness. They applaud.)*

AD LIBS. Ingenious! A stroke of genius! How droll! What will you think of next? Encore!

MISS MAPLE. Would you like to hear it again?

("Guests" nod their heads vigorously. Some sit.)

Mrs. Carlyle, if you'd be so kind.

LAURA. Here we go. One more time.

*(She snaps on **RADIO**. Only this time, the male voice is different. Deep, eerie, ominous.)*

RADIO. I accuse!

PETER. I accuse?

MISS MAPLE. That's not it.

CHANDLER. Get it like you had it before.

*(**LAURA** fools with the dial.)*

LAURA. Something's wrong with the dial.

RADIO. Chandler Marlowe –

CHANDLER. Me?

RADIO. Yes, you. I accuse you of a foul crime. You cannot escape your past.

*(As radio accuses characters in turn, all react nervously. **LAURA** steps back from console.)*

Looney Cheesecake.

LOUIS. That's Croissant. Louis Croissant.

RADIO. Remember that night in Shanghai? I accuse you of treachery. Rick and Laura Carlyle – what does the name "tulip" signify?

LAURA. Tulip?

RADIO. I accuse you of unforgivable deceit.

RICK. *(to **LAURA**)* How'd anyone find out about Tulip?

LAURA. Be quiet.

RADIO. Father White – why are you here at Ravenswood Manor? I accuse you of a sinister motive. Peter Flimsey – what actually happened on the cricket field at Eton? I accuse you of dishonor.

HAVERSHAM. Shall I set out the blue cheese fondue?

MISS MAPLE. Hold your tongue.

(*Which is what* **HAVERSHAM** *does, sticking out her tongue and holding it with her thumb and finger.*)

RADIO. Charity Haze – I accuse you of murder. None of you will escape. You will be punished. Miss Maple?

MISS MAPLE. (*without thinking*) Yes?

RADIO. What is the real secret of Ravenswood Manor?

MISS MAPLE. Is that all?

RADIO. That is all.

(*Sound of static.* **LAURA** *snaps off radio.*)

RICK. Uh, uh, you've outdone yourself, Miss Maple.

(*Feeble applause. "Guests" are uneasy. The radio accusations have hit home.*)

LAURA. (*nervously*) I'd like to go to my room now.

RICK. Not a bad idea I could do with a slap of aftershave.

MISS MAPLE. Through the hallway, up the stairs. You'll find your names on your door.

(*"Guests" move gloomily into hallway and out.* **LOUIS** *remains.*)

LOUIS. A most delightful interlude, Miss Maple.

MISS MAPLE. Thank you, Mr. *Moto.*

LOUIS. Please excuse me, but I have not yet seen my room. (**LOUIS** *bows his head and moves up center. He turns back.*) Do not let the voice on the radio frighten you. Remember. If you can keep your head while all around you are losing theirs, you'll be taller than they are. (*He exits upstage center.*)

HAVERSHAM. He doesn't seem deaf to me.

MISS MAPLE. Who?

HAVERSHAM. Mr. Cream Puff. You said he was deaf.

MISS MAPLE. *Deft,* deft. Not deaf.

HAVERSHAM. What about the blue cheese fondue?

MISS MAPLE. Will you stop talking about the fondue. (*moves to console, alarmed*) Who put that last tape…

HAVERSHAM. I thought you did. I can tell you one thing, Miss Maple. Your guests are shaking in their socks. I know a roomful of scared pigeons when I see them.

(Thunder. Room lights flicker.)

MISS MAPLE. The storm. Why isn't Rita here when I need her?

(RITA enters upstage center with hatbox.)

RITA. I'm here, Miss Maple.

MISS MAPLE. Why didn't you tell me about that tape? The one accusing my guests of dark crimes. I don't like surprises.

RITA. I don't know anything about it. I'm on my way to the motorboat to check supplies. If you'll excuse me.

(crosses to balcony doors, exits)

HAVERSHAM. I'd keep an eye on her if I was you.

MISS MAPLE. Well, you're not me. Come to the kitchen. I want to check on the fondue.

(MISS MAPLE exits downstage right. HAVERSHAM follows. Another roar of thunder followed by a dimming up and down of the lights. RICK enters from hallway.)

RICK. What time is dinner?

(RICK looks about, realizes he's alone. Shrugs. Sees tray, crosses to it. He sips some wine, nibbles at a biscuit. Suddenly he gives a cry — as if something were stuck in his throat. Drops wine glass. He staggers back in exaggerated fashion, clutching his throat. He staggers forward, back again. Forward. He dies in overdramatic fashion, hitting the floor with a spiraling wail. On cue, the "Guests" rush in from hallway, ad libbing alarm. Lights back to normal.)

AD LIBS. What was that cry?
Who cried out?
What's happened?
Sounded like Rick!

(**PETER** *and* **FATHER WHITE** *move left.* **LOUIS, LAURA** *move right.* **CHANDLER** *stands upstage center. All see the body sprawled on the floor.*)

LAURA. *(hand to her mouth)* It is *Rick.*

(**MISS MAPLE, HAVERSHAM** *enter downstage right.* **RITA** *enters from outside the room)*

MISS MAPLE. Who screamed?

("Guests" point to **RICK.** **CHANDLER** *moves to the corpse, kneels beside it, investigates.)*

PETER. Is he – dead?

CHANDLER. *(confirms)* Can't get any deader. (**CHANDLER** *picks up wine glass, sniffs.)*

FATHER WHITE. The radio voice. It said we'd be punished.

MISS MAPLE. I had nothing to do with that.

RITA. I have an important announcement to make.

PETER. About Rick Carlyle?

RITA. No, about the motorboat.

FATHER WHITE. What about it?

RITA. It's gone.

OTHERS. Gone?!

(Thunder. A figurine falls from the mantel. **HAVER-SHAM** *screams.)*

LAURA. Now what?

HAVERSHAM. A figurine fell off the mantel.

(**FATHER WHITE** *moves to the figurine, picks it up. It's broken in two.)*

FATHER WHITE. Broken.

LOUIS. I think I understand. Most classic. As each of us is "punished," a figurine will fall from the mantel. Nine in this room, nine figurines on the mantel.

RITA. Three.

LOUIS. Explain, please.

RITA. There aren't nine figurines on the mantel, there are only three.

LOUIS. Only three? Just like *The Three Musketeers,* my favorite novel. French, you know.

CHANDLER. Forget the figurines. We've got a dead man here. My guess is poison.

OTHERS. Poison!

CHANDLER. It means murder.

OTHERS. Murder!

MISS MAPLE. What are you going to do?

CHANDLER. I'm going to solve this case. I'll want to speak with the servants. The butler first.

MISS MAPLE. The butler?

(Others face out to audience to ask the vital question.)

OTHERS. The butler did it?

(Thunder. Lights fade fast, leaving the weekend party in near-silhouette as a musical dischord is struck on the piano to suggest impending doom.)

Scene Two

(AT RISE: Later. The storm howls outside Ravenswood Manor. Here and there a lamp glows in the empty room. Several moments pass and then, slowly – the bookcase swings open. A flashlight beam is seen and **FATHER WHITE** *cautiously enters, closes the entrance to the "secret passageway.")*

CHANDLER. *(offstage)* Hey, Flimsey! Where are you? Flimsey!

(Fast, **FATHER WHITE** *moves to the sofa, sits, putting the flashlight behind him.* **CHANDLER,** *his coat wet, enters.)*

FATHER WHITE. What are you doing out there in the storm?

CHANDLER. What do you think I'm doing? Hunting for clues, natch.

FATHER WHITE. Any clues you find out there will be all wet

CHANDLER. Wet, dry – what's the dif? Flimsey and me stretched out Carlyle in the wine cellar. He's colder than the heart of an I.R.S. agent.

FATHER WHITE. I fear Miss Maple's little "charade" has taken a nasty turn.

CHANDLER. Never saw a murder that wasn't nasty. I know nasty. Tell you something, padre. Fancy dumps like Ravenswood Manor are too rich for my blood. The mean streets are my beat.

FATHER WHITE. You work with your emotions, Chandler. *(taps his head)* I work with my intellect.

CHANDLER. As far as this case is concerned we're both out of work.

LAURA. *(enters upstage center)* Am I intruding?

FATHER WHITE. *(starts to rise)* No, no, my dear. Do join us.

LAURA. Don't get up.

(She moves downstage. **FATHER WHITE** *sits.)*

CHANDLER. Sorry about your tragedy, kid. Could you get any sleep?

LAURA. *(cheerfully)* Dropped off the minute my head hit the pillow.

CHANDLER. *(to audience)* Grief does that.

LAURA. I suppose you're wondering why I've taken Rick's demise so lightly.

CHANDLER. You ain't exactly used up a box of Kleenex. But who's checking?

LAURA. Truth is Rick and I have been estranged for some time. Would you like to hear about it?

FATHER WHITE. Not really.

CHANDLER. Naw.

LAURA. Since you insist. *(dramatic confession)* Rick was interested in another woman. I had a private investigator investigate her. Her name was Mabel Dupre.

CHANDLER. What is it now?

LAURA. What are you talking about?

CHANDLER. You said her name *was* Dupre. What does she call herself now?

LAURA. I imagine her name is still Mabel Dupre. Fascinating, I suppose, but unscrupulous. Such women usually are.

FATHER WHITE. Tsk, tsk. I can well understand the attraction. Mabel Dupre, the flame, Rick Carlyle, the moth.

CHANDLER. Only the moth got burned – bad.

LAURA. Badly.

CHANDLER. Huh?

LAURA. You said "bad." You meant "badly."

CHANDLER. You ain't exactly the grieving widow type, are you?

LAURA. I cry all the time. On the inside. Where it doesn't show.

FATHER WHITE. What does this Miss Dupre look like?

LAURA. I've never seen the cat, but I've heard her voice. On the telephone.

CHANDLER. What did she say?

LAURA. She said, "Hello, hello. Anybody there?" Then she hung up.

*(**MISS MAPLE** enters from downstage right.)*

MISS MAPLE. How can I ever apologize? Murder is so inconvenient. When I find out who's responsible for ruining my lovely party, I shall be most severe. If there's anything I cannot tolerate it's rudeness. Whoever murdered poor Mr. Carlyle did a rude thing.

LAURA. It was gross.

(**FLIMSEY** *enters upstage center.*)

PETER. Hi ho, everyone.

CHANDLER. I been looking for you, Flimsey. I thought you were going to give me a hand outside. For all we know the killer is out there prowling around.

MISS MAPLE. Do you think he might strike again?

CHANDLER. If he tries – *(holds up a fist)* I'll know how to handle him.

(**LOUIS** *enters downstage right.*)

LOUIS. If brute force were all, the tiger would not fear the scorpion.

CHANDLER. *(agitated)* Will you stop talking about bugs?

LOUIS. Why? Is it bugging you? (**LOUIS** *laughs at his own joke.*)

MISS MAPLE. I'm so worried.

CHANDLER. Don't be, little sister. Chandler Marlowe is on the job and murder is *my* business.

MISS MAPLE. What a comfort.

(*As* **CHANDLER** *sings,* **MISS MAPLE** *sits beside* **FATHER WHITE** *on the sofa.* **LOUIS** *steps in front of fireplace.* **LAURA** *sits in chair, left.* **PETER** *moves to desk.*)

SONG – MURDER IS MY BUSINESS

CHANDLER.

(sings)

MURDER IS MY BUSINESS
IT CAN'T BE DENIED
TO SAY THAT MY PROFESSION IS HOMICIDE
THE KILLER WILL FIND THERE IS NO HIDING
PLACE

BECAUSE CHANDLER MARLOWE IS NOW ON
THE CASE
YEAH, MURDER IS THE BUSINESS OF A GUY
WHO'S A PRIVATE EYE.

(spoken)

I wanted to be a detective because my old man was a detective. I admired him, y'know. He was smart.

OTHERS. *(spoken)* How smart?

CHANDLER. *(spoken)* He used to say, "Kid, dames is simple. Dames only understand two things: a slap in the mouth and a slug from a forty-five."

(sings)
BEIN' A DETECTIVE
WAS PART OF THE PLAN
TO FOLLOW IN THE FOOTSTEPS OF MY OLD MAN
I BOUGHT ME A TRENCHCOAT, BOUGHT ME A ROD
I LEARNED TO BE ROUGH WITH A TOUGH LITTLE BROAD
YEAH, CHANDLER MARLOWE, JUNIOR, WAS
    THE SON OF A PRIVATE EYE.

(spoken)

Next to my old man I got my inspiration from movies like *The Maltese Falcon.* Remember Alan Ladd? (**OTHERS** *nod.*) He was tough.

OTHERS. *(spoken)* How tough?

(**CHANDLER** *frowns at the interruption.*)

CHANDLER. *(spoken)* Who cared if he was only five feet tall and had to stand on an orange crate to kiss his leading lady? I loved the guy. *(sings)*

STARTED SEEIN' MOVIES WHEN I WAS THIRTEEN
I LOVED TO WATCH A MYST'RY UPON THE SCREEN
THE HARD-BOILED DETECTIVE, THE GOOD-LOOKING MOLL
LIKE HUMPHREY BOGART AND LAUREN BACALL
YEAH, MOVIES WERE THE PASSION OF A GUY
CALLED A PRIVATE EYE.

(spoken)

After the old man kicked off, I went into business for myself. A one-man detective agency with this on the door: CHANDLER MARLOWE: MURDER IS MY BUSINESS, I could never make a decision on taking a case until I had a shot of cheap whiskey, the cheaper the better. I kept a bottle in my desk, out of respect for my old man, *(mimes a toast)* Here's looking at you, kid. *(sings)*

OPENED UP AN OFFICE
RIGHT OFF MARKET STREET
THE TOWN OF SAN FRANCISCO BECAME MY BEAT
FROM FISHERMAN'S WHARF OUT TO GOLDEN GATE PARK
FROM OLD CHINATOWN TO THE TOP OF THE MARK
THE TOWN OF SAN FRANCISCO WAS THE BEAT
OF A PRIVATE EYE,

(spoken) Private eye, private ear. It's all the same to Chandler Marlowe, I take a case the same way I take a slug of hot lead, With a smile on my kisser. Twisted, but a smile. If there's gum on my shoe, I step on it. I'm tough, Like I said, Miss Maple, you ain't got nothing to worry about. Solving murders is a dirty job, but somebody's gotta do it. And I'm the guy, *(sings)*

MURDER IS MY BUSINESS
SO GIVE ME AWHILE
AND I WILL FIND THE KILLER OF RICK CARLYLE
THE MURDERER KNOWS THERE IS NO HIDING PLACE
BECAUSE CHANDLER MARLOWE IS NOW ON THE CASE,
YEAH, MURDER IS THE BUSINESS OF A GUY
WHO'S A PRIVATE EYE

CHANDLER. *(spoken)* Play it again, Sam. *(sings)*

MURDER IS THE BUSINESS OF A
GUY WHO'S A PRIVATE EYE.

MISS MAPLE. I shall rely on you implicitly, Mr. Marlowe.

LOUIS. No need to rely on Chandler Marlowe. Louis Croissant will presently name the murderer of the once semi-famous Rick Carlyle.

(**OTHERS** *are agog by* **LOUIS**' *announcement.*)

MISS MAPLE. Mr. Crouton, I take it you are about to shed light on this terrible affair at Ravenswood Manor?

LOUIS. Patience. All will be revealed. Even now the name of the killer is on the tip of my lung.

CHANDLER. The guy we need here is Pharoah Link.

MISS MAPLE. Who?

CHANDLER. Top detective on the Frisco force.

LAURA. You're all babbling. I know who killed Rick. Why won't anyone believe me? Mabel Dupre.

PETER. Why would she kill your husband?

LAURA. Rick preferred me and, obviously, told her so. The motive is revenge.

FATHER WHITE. What proof do you have?

LAURA. Who needs proof? I've got something better than proof.

CHANDLER. What's better than proof?

LAURA. *(into audience)* A woman's intuition.

LOUIS. We must get our choo-choo train back on its track. I am solving this case. The clue is in the recording. This just came to me like a bolt out of the glue. The killer knew each of us – intimately.

FATHER WHITE. If you mean those nasty accusations, I have no idea what the radio voice was talking about. I am here only because I was invited.

LOUIS. Find out who made the recording and we have the murderer.

LAURA. That's your solution?

CHANDLER. Pretty thin.

MISS MAPLE. I thought you were going to give us a name. I'm disappointed in you, Leonard.

LOUIS. Louis. Louis

PETER. I'm afraid Mr. Cornbread does get carried away. He does that in his writings, too. Never could make any sense out of his nonsense. One finds more clarity in a fortune cookie.

FATHER WHITE. Do we fully grasp the seriousness of the situation? Cut off from the mainland, the raging storm.

LAURA. A face at the window walking around.

PETER. No boat

FATHER WHITE. I think it would be wise if none of us ate or drank anything until morning.

LOUIS. If we are still – alive.

*(Thunder. All react to **LOUIS**'s dire words.)*

PETER. I don't think we have anything to worry about when it comes to food and drink. The poison was not in the sherry. *(All react.)* Stand up, please, Mrs. Carlyle. *(She does.)* Step aside, please.

*(She does. **PETER** takes out a magnifying glass.)*

CHANDLER. A magnifying glass? You've got to be kidding.

PETER. Magnifying glasses have become quite sophisticated since the days of London fog and hansom cabs. This one, for example, magnifies twenty times. It can also indentify odors.

(All sniff at the atmosphere.)

LOUIS. Yes. Someone in this room has halitosis.

MISS MAPLE. Amazing.

PETER. *(moves in front of the chair)* One should never be taken in by appearances. It's a capital mistake to theorize before one has all the evidence.

CHANDLER. So?

PETER. If you'll all look here, you'll see what I mean.

*(All move to the chair. **PETER** points to a spot in the upholstery.)*

PETER. There's a spot.

*(**LAURA** takes the glass, studies the chair.)*

See it?

LAURA. Why, it looks like a little needle.

PETER. Correct.

CHANDLER. Give me a look.

(*He takes the glass, looks. Each person has a turn.*)

PETER. Rick Carlyle was murdered by a poisoned dart.

ALL. Dart?

PETER. (*moves toward painting*) I discovered the dart about an hour ago. Since the dart entered the body at a downward angle, I surmised it came from the painting. Or rather, a hole in the wall.

(**CHANDLER** *crosses to the portrait, studies it.*)

CHANDLER. You're right. One eyeball is missing.

FATHER WHITE. We're up against a clever killer.

PETER. Either clever, or – mad. How do we know some lunatic didn't get wind of this weekend party, and decided to have a murderous lark?

LAURA. (*points*) Do you realize I was sitting in that chair?

MISS MAPLE. Good heavens, you might have been scratched!

PETER. I removed the dart, analyzed the poison, and returned the miniature weapon for the purpose of rec-reating the murder method. Without the poison it's harmless.

CHANDLER. I'll give you credit, Flimsey. You're no man's fool.

PETER. I appreciate that, Chandler.

CHANDLER. I still think we ought to case the island.

PETER. I'm ready.

CHANDLER. Let's go.

(*He crosses to the doors.* **PETER** *removes the dart.*)

MISS MAPLE. I'm terrified. What man could have done such a thing?

PETER. Aren't you forgetting something, Miss Maple?

MISS MAPLE. What?

PETER. Poison is a woman's weapon.

MISS MAPLE. I'm a woman.

PETER. I know.

(**MISS MAPLE** *gasps at the implication.*)

CHANDLER. Come on, before the killer gets away.

(*He exits into the storm.* **PETER** *follows.*)

MISS MAPLE. I should see to matters in the kitchen, but I'm frightened of every shadow.

LOUIS. I would be glad to offer my protection, Miss Maple.

MISS MAPLE. Thank you, Leroy. (*exits downstage right*)

LOUIS. (*follows*) While we're in the kitchen, do you think we might scare up a baloney sandwich? (*He exits.*)

LAURA. They're all a bunch of dolts. I tell you, the killer is Mabel Dupre. She's here in this house. I know it. I feel it.

FATHER WHITE. It's a possibility.

LAURA. You agree with my theory?

FATHER WHITE. I don't "disagree" with it. It's an old story. A man infatuated with a woman who can destroy him. It's happened before, you know. Many, many times. (*He sings.*)

SONG – THE MOTH TO THE FLAME

FATHER WHITE. (*cont.*)
THERE ONCE WAS A MAN WITH LONG TRESSES.
CALLED SAMSON, OF BIBLICAL FAME.
BUT HE GOT CUT SHORT BY DELILAH.
THE MOTH TO THE FLAME.

THERE ONCE WAS A HANDSOME BULLFIGHTER
THEY SAY "DON JOSE" WAS HIS NAME.
THE BULL THAT HE GOT WAS FROM CARMEN.
THE MOTH TO THE FLAME.

SO BEWARE, SO BEWARE.
IF YOU FIND THAT YOUR HEART IS AFLAME
JUST BE CAREFUL YOU DON'T FLY TOO CLOSE TO THE FIRE
AND GET BURNED LIKE A MOTH TO THE FLAME.

LAURA.

> WE'VE ALL HEARD OF SLY CLEOPATRA
> MARK ANTONY SHE TRIED TO CLAIM.
> SHE SAID, "COME AND PLAY ON THE SPHINX, DEAR!"
> THE MOTH TO THE FLAME.
>
> IT'S SAID IN THE CITY OF PARIS
> DUBARRY WAS CREME-DE-LA-CREME
> THEN ONE DAY SHE CURDLED KING LOUIE
> THE MOTH TO THE FLAME

BOTH.

> SO BEWARE, SO BEWARE
> IF YOU FIND THAT YOUR HEART IS AFLAME
> JUST BE CAREFUL YOU DON'T FLY TOO CLOSE TO THE FIRE
> AND GET BURNED LIKE A MOTH TO THE FLAME.

FATHER WHITE.

> YOU'VE HEARD OF THAT SPY FOR THE GERMANS?
> TO STEAL SECRET PLANS WAS HER AIM.
> THE ARMY ALL KNEW MATA HARI.
> THE MOTH TO THE FLAME.
> REMEMBER KING KONG IN THE MOVIES?
> A PASSIONATE BEAST HE BECAME.
> HE SIMPLY WENT "APE" FOR FAY WRAY, CHUM.
> THE MOTH TO THE FLAME.

BOTH.

> SO BEWARE, SO BEWARE.
> IF YOU FIND THAT YOUR HEART IS AFLAME
> JUST BE CAREFUL YOU DON'T FLY TOO CLOSE TO THE FIRE
> AND GET BURNED LIKE A MOTH TO THE FLAME.

LAURA.

> IF YOU ARE A SAILOR, TAKE WARNING
> WHEN TEMPESTS YOU'RE TRYING TO TAME
> WATCH OUT FOR THE SONG OF THE SIRENS
> THE MOTH TO THE FLAME.
> IF YOU'RE IN THE GARDEN OF EDEN
> TELL ADAM, "GET WISE TO THE GAME.
> DON'T BITE ON THAT APPLE FROM EVE, PAL."
> THE MOTH TO THE FLAME.

BOTH.

SO BEWARE, SO BEWARE
IF YOU FIND THAT YOUR HEART IS AFLAME.
JUST BE CAREFUL YOU DON'T FLY TOO CLOSE TO THE FIRE
AND GET BURNED LIKE A MOTH TO THE FLAME.

LAURA. I never thought of Mabel Dupre as a Delilah or a Cleopatra. As far as I'm concerned, she's a snake in the grass.

FATHER WHITE. We'll need more than your intuition, Mrs. Carlyle. *(indicated painting)* It took a lot of lung power to propel the poisoned dart and unless your Miss Dupre is an opera singer or a weight lifter, I don't believe she could have done it.

LAURA. Then you think the killer is a male?

FATHER WHITE. Time will tell.

LAURA. *(alarmed)* If your theory is correct, you could be the killer. Or Peter Flimsey, or Chandler Marlowe. Or Louis. You're all men. Sort of.

FATHER WHITE. *(trying to calm her)* Laura, Laura. Calm yourself.

LAURA. Stay away from me!

(She hurries out downstage right. Sound of storm. The lights flicker up and down. **FATHER WHITE** *picks up flashlight, checks the doors to ascertain that he's alone, moves to bookshelves, pulls them aside so he can enter the secret passageway.* **LAURA** *sneaks back in, stands downstage right, observing. Lights back to normal. When* **FATHER WHITE** *is gone and the bookcase back in position,* **LAURA** *moves to it, runs her hands over the shelves.)*

LAURA. There has to be a button or a lever somewhere. Where is it? Where? Where?

*(***RITA*** enters upstage center with her hat box.)*

RITA. *(looks around)* I thought I heard you talking to someone, Mrs. Carlyle.

LAURA. *(moves downstage left)* I do that when I'm nervous.

RITA. Would you like a sedative? *(puts down hat box)*

LAURA. Sleep is the last thing I want. At least when I'm awake I know I'm alive.

RITA. Miss Maple was so counting on a fun weekend.

LAURA. It's a raging success. If you have a macabre sense of humor.

RITA. I want to confide in someone.

LAURA. What about?

RITA. Haversham. She's on parole. Imprisoned because of some unpleasantness with a hatchet.

LAURA. *(thinks)* Haversham? Haversham? Hatchet? Hatchet? Of course! I recall the case.

RITA. Be on guard.

LAURA. I appreciate your telling me.

> (**RITA** *turns, start to exit downstage right.*)

Rita.

> (**RITA** *turns.*)

Don't forget your hat box.

> (**LAURA** *picks it up, holds it out.* **RITA** *suddenly realizes she doesn't have her hat box, runs to it and snatches it away.*)

RITA. Keep your hands off of it! It's mine! Mine! *(calms down)* I suppose you think it's strange the way I never let this hat box out of my sight.

> (**LAURA** *is convinced* **RITA** *is bonkers.*)

LAURA. No, no, honest The thought never crossed my mind. It's a, uh, "lovely" hat box.

RITA. *(moves the hat box from* **LAURA** *'s point of view)* I won't open it!

LAURA. *(uneasy)* Okay by me.

> *(sound of helicopter overheard)*

RITA. *(looks up)* What's that?

LAURA. I don't know. It could be an airplane.

RITA. It's too low for an airplane.

> (**MISS MAPLE** *and* **LOUIS** *enter from downstage right.*)

MISS MAPLE. It's a helicopter!

LAURA. Helicopter?

MISS MAPLE. Undoubtedly a police helicopter. We're saved!

(**CHANDLER** *and* **PETER** *appear at the doors.*)

CHANDLER. You ought to get a look at this. Wow!

PETER. It's over the house. You can see the lights through the rain and fog.

(**LOUIS, MISS MAPLE, RITA, LAURA** *join the men at the door, look offstage.*)

MISS MAPLE. Is it the police?

CHANDLER. Don't know, but they put a ladder down. I saw it swinging in the glow.

LAURA. Ladder? You mean they're dropping someone down in this weather?

LOUIS. Who would be foolhardy enough to descend to a house of murder?

CHARITY. Charity Haze, that's who.

(*All turn to see* **CHARITY** *standing downstage right, an incredibly capable and attractive young woman in a form-fitting raincoat, helmet and goggles.*)

CHANDLER. Charity, baby, you remember me, Chandler Marlowe. We met at Mardi Gras in New Orleans. I'd know you anywhere.

CHARITY. Charity Haze isn't your ordinary face in the crowd. (*She removes goggles and helmet revealing a gorgeous head of hair.*)

MISS MAPLE. I don't understand. A helicopter?

CHARITY. I missed the boat. This might be ungracious of me, but I could do with a hot bath.

RITA. I'll prepare one. (*exits upstage center*)

MISS MAPLE. I'm your hostess, my dear. (*introductions*)
This is Mr. Peter Flimsey, and this is Mr. Lousy Crackers, and –

CHARITY. Could we hold the introductions 'til after I've had my bath?

MISS MAPLE. Whatever you say, Charity. I'll show you to your room. You live up to your reputation.

(They move upstage center.)

CHARITY. Could I get a glass of sherry and a biscuit?

(They're out.)

CHANDLER. *(admiringly)* What a girl.

LOUIS. Remarkable young woman.

PETER. Exceptional. *(looks at **LAURA** who is wide-eyed)* What's the matter with you, Laura?

LAURA. *(points after **CHARITY**)* That voice! I'd recognize that voice anywhere! Mabel Dupre!

CHANDLER. Mabel's becoming an obsession, baby.

LOUIS. It's not possible for a new arrival to murder Rick and then ascend into the sky like a bird.

CHANDLER. Louis' making sense. For a change.

LAURA. Men! Bah!

LOUIS. I believe the murderer is one of us in this room. *(points an accusing finger to each)* You…you…you…you could be the murderer…and that is just the tip of the ice cube.

PETER. Yes, because you're leaving out one important point. What's the motive for the crime?

LOUIS. *(to audience)* That will be revealed in the second act.

CHANDLER. You're talking through your hat. I'm sticking with my original suspicion. If it's good enough for a mystery novel, it's good enough for the real thing.

PETER. The butler? Hmmm. You might be right, Chandler. But can we be sure?

*(As those onstage sing, **OTHERS** return in musical comedy style until **ENTIRE CAST** [including **STAFF**] is onstage. All take part in this Act One finale.)*

SONG – THE BUTLER DID IT

(NOTE: The first chorus is divided among the characters Onstage, roughly into three groups.)

FIRST GROUP.

> PERHAPS THE BUTLER DID IT.
> PERHAPS THE BUTLER DID IT.
> HE'S THE ONE WHO CAUSED THIS MURDEROUS AFFAIR.
> IT MUST HAVE BEEN THE BUTLER!
> IT MUST HAVE BEEN THE BUTLER!
> ALTHOUGH I HAVEN'T SEEN A BUTLER ANYWHERE.

SECOND GROUP.

> OF COURSE THE BUTLER DID IT!
> OF COURSE THE BUTLER DID IT!
> HE'S THE ONE WHO CAUSED THIS FRIGHTFUL FOLDEROL.
> IT MUST HAVE BEEN THE BUTLER.
> IT MUST HAVE BEEN THE BUTLER!
> THOUGH I HAVEN'T SEEN A BUTLER HERE AT ALL.

ALL.

> EV'RY GUEST WHO'S BEEN INVITED
> IS SUSPICIOUS AS CAN BE.
> WELL, I DON'T LIKE TO CONDEMN,
> BUT IT MUST BE ONE OF THEM
> FOR I ABSOLUTELY KNOW IT ISN'T ME.

THIRD GROUP.

> I KNOW THE BUTLER DID IT!
> I KNOW THE BUTLER DID IT!
> THOUGH IT SOUNDS, I KNOW, LIKE SUCH AN OLD CLICHE
> IT HAD TO BE THE BUTLER,
> IT ALWAYS IS THE BUTLER!
> THOUGH I HAVEN'T SEEN A BUTLER HERE TODAY.

WOMEN. *(including FEMALE STAFF)*

> *(second chorus)*
> I KNOW THE BUTLER DID IT
> I KNOW THE BUTLER DID IT.
> HE'S THE ONE WHO CAUSED THIS HIDEOUS
> DISGRACE.
> IT HAD TO BE THE BUTLER
> IT HAD TO BE THE BUTLER!
> ALTHOUGH I'VE NEVER MET THE BUTLER FACE-TO-FACE.

MEN. *(including MALE STAFF)*
>I KNOW THE BUTLER DID IT.
>I KNOW THE BUTLER DID IT.
>DON'T KNOW WHY WE DIDN'T THINK OF IT BEFORE.
>IT HAD TO BE THE BUTLER
>IT HAD TO BE THE BUTLER!
>THOUGH A BUTLER DIDN'T GREET US AT THE DOOR.

ALL.
>EV'RY GUEST WHO'S BEEN INVITED
>IS SUSPICIOUS AS CAN BE.
>THOUGH IT'S AWFUL TO DISCUSS
>WELL, IT MIGHT BE ONE OF US.
>BUT I DEFINITELY KNOW IT ISN'T ME.
>WE KNOW THE BUTLER DID IT!
>WE KNOW THE BUTLER DID IT!
>THOUGH IT SOUNDS, WE KNOW, LIKE SUCH AN OLD CLICHE
>IT HAD TO BE THE BUTLER
>IT ALWAYS IS THE BUTLER
>THOUGH WE HAVEN'T SEEN A BUTLER HERE TODAY.
>IT HAD TO BE THE BUTLER
>IT ALWAYS IS THE BUTLER
>ON THAT POINT WE ALL AGREE.
>WE KNOW WITHOUT
>THE SHADOW OF A DOUBT
>THAT IT DEFINITELY,
>POSITIVELY,
>ABSOLUTELY
>WASN'T ME!

(**CAST** *freezes in position, staring out into the audience. Blackout. Almost immediately, during audience applause, the general stage lighting returns.* **CAST** *continues to stare into audience until the applause fades. Audience waits for some dramatic announcement and the* **CAST** *makes it.*)

CAST. Intermission.

ACT II

Scene One

(Entr'acte music [Prior to II, I])

(OPTIONAL OPENING: **STAFF** *enters and sing a brief reprise of Murder, Mystery, Mayhem, exits.)*

(AT RISE: Later. An occasional gush of wind is heard. **MISS MAPLE** *enters downstage right.* **CHANDLER** *is behind her. As the two converse,* **MISS MAPLE** *sits on the sofa,* **CHANDLER** *stands left.)*

MISS MAPLE. I'm *terribly* disappointed in Louis Crumbcake. I expected better of him. He's full of cold tea.

CHANDLER. Never read much of his stuff. Too soft for me. I like my crime hard-boiled.

MISS MAPLE. Murder is not an egg, Chandler. *(smiles)* You say you knew Charity Haze from the past?

CHANDLER. Louisiana. Mardi Gras. I was dressed like a gorilla and she was dressed like a jungle princess. It was fate.

MISS MAPLE. How romantic.

CHANDLER. Actually it was muggy. Got mildew on my gum-shoes.

MISS MAPLE. *(sighs)* I can't stop thinking about Mr. Carlyle. I had Rita throw an embroidered bedsheet over his corpse.

CHANDLER. Embroidered? That's what I call class.

MISS MAPLE. It was the least I could do under the circumstances.

*(***CHARITY*** enters upstage center.)*

CHARITY. I feel like a human being, thanks to that hot tub.

*(***CHANDLER*** gives a long, low whistle.)*

CHANDLER. You look like a human being, baby. My kind of human being. A jungle princess.

CHARITY. You still look like a gorilla.

MISS MAPLE. We were talking about you, Charity.

(**CHARITY** *moves downstage.*)

CHARITY. Were you?

MISS MAPLE. Don't be offended, but I must admit your type of writing is a bit, uh, too "forceful" for my taste. However, I realize you're quite popular. You must know something I don't. You certainly know how to handle men. What's your secret, my dear?

CHANDLER. It ain't exactly a secret. Go on, doll baby. Tell Miss Maple what makes you a package of dynamite. *(to audience)* As if I didn't know.

SONG – *I KNOW MY STUFF*

CHARITY.

WHY DO WEAK MEN TRIP AND STUMBLE?
WHY DO STRONG MEN CHIP AND CRUMBLE?
WHEN THEY SEE ME USE MY POWDER PUFF?
THE REASON IS:
I KNOW MY STUFF.

HE'LL BECOME A REAL GO-GETTER
WHEN I WEAR A WELL-FILLED SWEATER
CHANCES ARE HE'LL WANNA TREAT ME ROUGH.
THE REASON IS:
I KNOW MY STUFF.

I'VE GOT SWEET LIPS.
THEY'RE REALLY-A-TREAT LIPS.
BECAUSE THEY'RE NEAT LIPS.
TURN-ON-THE-HEAT LIPS!

WHEN I MEET WITH MY STOCKBROKER
FOR A LITTLE GAME OF POKER
WHY IS IT HE'LL NEVER CALL BY BLUFF?
THE REASON IS:
I KNOW MY STUFF.

(second chorus)
IF HE WANTS TO QUOTE SOME SHAKESPHERE
I WON'T SAY, "PUT ON THE BRAKES, DEAR"

I WILL ONLY SAY, "LEAD ON, MACDUFF."
THE REASON IS:
I KNOW MY STUFF.

WHEN A FELLA WANTS TO WRESTLE
I BECOME A WEAKER VESSEL.
I WILL ALWAYS LET HIM THINK HE'S TOUGH.
THE REASON IS:
I KNOW MY STUFF.
HAVE I GOT LIPS.
YOU'LL LIKE 'EM A LOT LIPS.
BECAUSE THEY'RE HOT LIPS,
ONE-HUNDRED-WATT LIPS!

WHEN I UNDULATE MY BODY
KINDA LIKE SCHEHERAZADE, (SHAW-HAIR-UH-ZODDY)
SEEMS THE FELLAS NEVER GET ENOUGH.
THE REASON IS:
I KNOW MY STUFF.

I'M SO PERSUASIVE,
THAT'S A FACT.
I GOT DIRTY HARRY TO CLEAN UP HIS ACT.
I KNOW MY STUFF.

MISS MAPLE. You're a modern young woman, Charity. I salute you.

CHARITY. *(tosses a salute)* Thanks.

MISS MAPLE. I was annoyed when you didn't arrive on the boat, then I was relieved.

CHARITY. Relieved? How come?

MISS MAPLE. I mean – now that we're all targets for some deranged killer.

CHARITY. *(to* **CHANDLER***)* What are you doing about it?

CHANDLER. Keeping calm.

*(***FATHER WHITE*** enters downstage right.)*

FATHER WHITE. I'm not keeping calm. I've been in the wine cellar. There's a body down there.

MISS MAPLE. Naturally there's a body there.

CHANDLER. Rick Carlyle.

FATHER WHITE. *He's dead! Really* dead.

CHANDLER. You been sampling the wares in that cellar?

FATHER WHITE. I'm not drunk. *(distraught)* I thought it was part of the game, part of the charade. I expected Rick to show up later and tell us it was all a joke. But it's not a joke. Ha, ha It's *murda!* Ha, ha.

CHARITY. Sit down, Father. You're going weak in the knee-caps.

(**FATHER WHITE** *moves in front of sofa, talking as he crosses.*)

Is it any wonder? Fun and games are one thing –

CHANDLER. Yeah, yeah, we know. Murder's something else.

FATHER WHITE. I don't know what to believe anymore. *(He sits in left center chair.)*

MISS MAPLE. I quite understand your distress.

FATHER WHITE. *(moaning)* He's dead…dead…

(**PETER** *enters from outside.*)

CHANDLER. You're repeating yourself, Padre.

PETER. What's the matter with him?

CHARITY. He just discovered the corpse in the wine cellar is the real article.

PETER. You mean he didn't know?

FATHER WHITE. Nooooo…

MISS MAPLE. I've asked the others to join me. I do wish they'd get here.

(**LOUIS** *enters upstage center.*)

LOUIS. When my honorable hostess requests, her honorable guest complies.

MISS MAPLE. Oh, it's you, Mr. Spade. *(scoffs)* You honestly believe the radio voice is the murderer? What rubbish. What a juvenile deduction. Preposterous.

LOUIS. Come, come, Miss Maple. We all have the jitters. Not to mention the heebie-jeebies and the fidgets. You, in particular, are a bungle of nerves. It's as plain as the chins on your face.

(**LAURA** *enters upstage center. Cold, determined, convinced* **CHARITY** *is* **MABEL DUPRE.**)

MISS MAPLE. There you are, Laura, dear. Sit by me.

LAURA. I'd rather stand. *(She strides to the fireplace, turns with her arms folded. She glares at* **CHARITY.**)

CHARITY. *(to others)* Why is she looking at me like that? *(to* **LAURA**) What have I done?

MISS MAPLE. Ladies and gentlemen, I must apologize for the strange turn of events at Ravenswood Manor. *(stands)* But no one must think I would stoop so low as to engineer this "misfortune" with Mr. Carlyle.

CHARITY. You mean we might suspect you were out to publicize your new chain of bookstores with something kinky?

(*Guests look innocently around the room.* **CHARITY** *has let the cat out.*)

MISS MAPLE. So. *(flat)* You all knew about the bookstores?

AD LIBS. Well, uh,

That is –

Uh, uh –

PETER. What if we did know? No harm done, is there?

MISS MAPLE. Until now my reputation as a hostess has been impeccable. We have no choice but to remain on the island until morning. I intend to take advantage of every moment. I will not bow to any sinister force. *(hand up for emphasis) The* charade *will continue!*

(*Impressed by her fervor,* **GUESTS** *politely applaud.*)

I want the killer found.

FATHER WHITE. Well and good, Miss Maple, but we're mystery writers, not the police.

MISS MAPLE. I've invited you here because you're supposedly the best in your field. *Prove it.*

CHANDLER. If all else fails we could get a pretty good yarn out of this. I got my title already – *Murder Walks the Fog.*

LOUIS. *Island of Evil.*

FATHER WHITE. *Mystery in San Francisco Bay.*

CHARITY. *The Corpse in the Wine Cellar.*

LAURA. *One Mad Weekend.*

MISS MAPLE. The sooner the killer is caught, the sooner we can hand the beast over to the proper authorities. To assure you that I'm not frivolous in my desire to catch the monster, I will award an honorarium to the one who smokes him out. $25,000.

ALL. $25,000!

CHANDLER. That's some honor…honor…whatever that word was.

(**MISS MAPLE** *crosses downstage right, turns.*)

MISS MAPLE. You have until sunrise. *(She exits.)*

CHARITY. She means it.

CHANDLER. *(rubbing his hands in gleeful fashion)* Yeah.

CHARITY. I'm betting on the male of the species. He's our killer.

PETER. I can't agree, Miss Haze. No *male* detective would.

FATHER WHITE. Quite so. When in doubt – look for the woman in the case.

LOUIS. Oui! As they say in my country – *"Cherchez La Femme!"* French, you know.

CHARITY. Cherchez La who?

PETER. *(with great feeling)* It was that famous detective Monsieur Jackal in Dumas' The *Mochicans of Paris* who first used the phrase. Forever saying – *Cherchez la femme!*

LAURA. This isn't getting us anywhere.

PETER. Surely, you all know that Monsieur Jackal was the literary ancestor of all the great ferrets from Victor Hugo's Javert –

CHARITY. Victor who?

LOUIS. Not "Who." *Hugo.*

FATHER WHITE. What's a ferret?

PETER. Your education in the history of detectives is sadly lacking. But what does it matter? *Cherchez –*

MALE DETECTIVES. *La Femme!*

SONG – CHERCHEZ LA FEMME

PETER.

> CHERCHEZ LA FEMME,
> MY FRIEND,
> JUST WHO COULD THE GUILTY ONE BE?
> CHERCHEZ LA FEMME,
> MY FRIEND,
> THE GUILTY ONE'S SELDOM A HE.
> YOU WANT TO KNOW JUST WHO THE CRIMINAL IS
> THE ONE THE JURY SHOULD CONDEMN?
> THE SEARCH IS THROUGH,
> MY FRIEND,
> THE ANSWER IS CHERCHEZ LA FEMME.
> CHERCHEZ LA FEMME,
> MY FRIEND,
> JUST WHO COULD THE GUILTY ONE BE?
> CHERCHEZ LA FEMME,
> MY FRIEND,
> THE GUILTY ONE'S SELDOM A HE.
> YOU WANT TO KNOW WHO DID THE GENTLEMAN IN
> WHO STABBED HIM WITH A BUTCHER KNIFE?
> THE SEARCH IS THROUGH,
> MY FRIEND,
> THE ANSWER IS CHERCHEZ LA WIFE.

FATHER WHITE.

> CHERCHEZ LA FEMME,
> MY FRIEND,
> JUST WHO COULD THE GUILTY ONE BE?
> CHERCHEZ LA FEMME,
> MY FRIEND,
> THE GUILTY ONE'S SELDOM A HE.
> YOU WANT TO KNOW WHO DID THE GENTLEMAN IN
> WITH ARS'NIC IN HIS LEMONADE?
> THE SEARCH IS THROUGH,
> MY FRIEND
> THE ANSWER IS CHERCHEZ LA MAID.

CHANDLER.

> CHERCHEZ LA FEMME,
> MY FRIEND,
> JUST WHO COULD THE GUILTY ONE BE?
> CHERCHEZ LA FEMME,
> MY FRIEND,
> THE GUILTY ONE'S SELDOM A HE.
> YOU WANT TO KNOW WHO DID THE GENTLEMAN IN
> WHO PUSHED HIM OFF THAT WATERFALL?
> THE SEARCH IS THROUGH,
> MY FRIEND,
> THE ANSWER IS CHERCHEZ LA DOLL.

LOUIS.

> CHERCHEZ LA FEMME,
> MY FRIEND,
> JUST WHO COULD THE GUILTY ONE BE?
> CHERCHEZ LA FEMME,
> MY FRIEND,
> THE GUILTY ONE'S SELDOM A HE.
> YOU WANT TO KNOW WHO DID THE GENTLEMAN IN
> WHO PUT THE BOMB IN HIS VALISE?
> THE SEARCH IS THROUGH,
> MY FRIEND,
> THE ANSWER IS CHERCHEZ LA NIECE.

PETER.

> CHERCHEZ LA FEMME,
> MY FRIEND,
> JUST WHO COULD THE GUILTY ONE BE?
> CHERCHEZ LA FEMME,
> MY FRIEND,
> THE GUILTY ONE'S SELDOM A HE.
> YOU WANT TO KNOW WHO DID THE GENTLEMAN IN
> JUST WHEN HE THOUGHT ROMANCE WAS HIS?
> THE SEARCH IS THROUGH,
> MY FRIEND,
> THE ANSWER IS CHERCHEZ LA MS.

ALL.

> *(becomes "A Chorus Line" / Rockettes Finale)*
>
> CHERCHEZ LA FEMME,
> MY FRIEND,
> JUST WHO COULD THE GUILTY ONE BE?
> CHERCHEZ LA FEMME,
> MY FRIEND,
> THE GUILTY ONE'S SELDOM A HE.
> YOU WANT TO KNOW JUST WHO THE CRIMINAL IS
> THE ONE THE JURY SHOULD CONDEMN?
> THE SEARCH IS THROUGH,
> MY FRIEND,
> THE SEARCH IS THROUGH,
> MY FRIEND,
> THE SEARCH IS THROUGH,
> MY FRIEND,
> THE ANSWER IS CHERCHEZ LA FEMME.
>
> *(**MALE DETECTIVES** are pleased with their various observations about lady villains. They shake hands, slap each other on the shoulder.)*

LOUIS. *(to audience)* This song should have been given to me as a solo. I must speak with the director.

CHARITY. *(to **LAURA**)* They're like little boys, aren't they?

LAURA. How dare you speak to me!

CHARITY. You got some kind of problem?

LAURA. You can't fool me!

CHARITY. *(to **MALE DETECTIVES**)* What's the matter with her?

LAURA. *(to **MALE DETECTIVES**)* Why are you standing there? Do something! *(points)* There's the killer. She's the one! Mabel Dupre!

FATHER WHITE. Here we go again.

CHANDLER. Easy, Mrs. Carlyle. She ain't the Dupre dame. Take my word for it. It's Charity Haze.

LAURA. *(advancing on **CHARITY**)* Don't let the phony wig fool you. She's clever. She's devious. She's got lung power. It's Mabel, I tell you.

CHARITY. Mabel? Mabel?

FATHER WHITE. You're making a mistake. You're not yourself.

LAURA. Take off that wig!

(With that she grabs **CHARITY** *by the hair. Aghast* **MALE DETECTIVES** *separate, left and right out of the battle range.* **CHARITY** *and* **LAURA** *struggle in front of sofa.* **HAVERSHAM** *pops in downright, looks.)*

HAVERSHAM. Miss Maple ain't going to like this. *(turns to exit)* Miss Maple! Miss Maple! *(She's out.)*

CHARITY. Ow, ow, ow!!!

LAURA. You homewrecker!

CHARITY. You're crazy!

LAURA. Give me that wig!

CHARITY. Ow, ow, ow!

*(***LAURA** *continues to pull at* **CHARITY,** *who protests loudly. Others move around trying to stop the fracas.)*

FATHER WHITE. Laura, control yourself!

CHANDLER. Let me handle this.

LOUIS. The plot sickens.

PETER. Do something, Chandler!

LAURA. Give me that wig!

CHARITY. It's not a wig!

*(***CHARITY** *winds up and socks* **LAURA** *on the chin. She falls back into the left center chair.)*

It's my own hair, you idiot.

LAURA. *(calms down, rubs her cheek)* The joke's on me.

(At this point positions are as follows: **LAURA** *in the chair,* **CHARITY** *in front of the sofa.* **CHANDLER** *and* **PETER** *stage left,* **LOUIS** *and* **FATHER WHITE** *stage right.)*

CHARITY. What was that all about?

LOUIS. She mistook you for her arch rival. The infamous Mabel Dupre.

CHANDLER. You still pack a mean wallop, Sugar.

CHARITY. *(blows on her knuckles)* I can take care of myself, Chandler. I understand the recording accused me of murder.

CHANDLER. Yeah.

CHARITY. Easily explained.

LAURA. How?

CHARITY. Since I've never actually murdered anyone, anyone real, that is, the recording had to mean a popular character in one of my books – Jumbo.

CHANDLER. A great gumshoe.

CHARITY. I got bored with him and knocked him off. In print. There was a public outcry. Critics said I "murdered" Jumbo.

PETER. In much the same manner, Doyle caused a sensation when he killed off Sherlock Holmes.

LAURA. Interesting, but so what?

LOUIS. A most interesting explanation. I suggest other possibilities.

FATHER WHITE. What other possibilities?

LOUIS. When all is darkest, the cricket will chirp and that is the fly in the oatmeal.

CHANDLER. There he goes again – talking about bugs.

(**RITA** *enters downstage right. There's an afghan over her arm.*)

RITA. It's getting chilly. I thought someone might need an afghan. I'll put them in the bedrooms, too. *(puts the afghan over the sofa back)*

LAURA. We won't be doing much sleeping.

RITA. Gets quite chilly on the island. *(She exits upstage center.)*

FATHER WHITE. First time I've seen her without her hat box.

LOUIS. Curious you should mention the hat box. It recalls The Case of the Headless Horseman.

CHANDLER. A famous case. A jockey was murdered by his girlfriend during the Kentucky Derby.

CHARITY. Why did they call him the Headless Horseman?

CHANDLER. What would fit in a hatbox? Besides a hat, that is. *(Pregnant pause as the terrible implication registers.)*

LAURA. You mean –

FATHER WHITE. You mean –

CHARITY. You mean –

LOUIS. Miss Eyelesbarrow looks amazingly like the missing girlfriend, a female addicted to hats. I noticed the similarity as soon as I entered Ravenswood Manor.

LAURA. I'm not worried about the missing girlfriend. I'm worried about the jockey's missing-

FATHER WHITE. Don't say it, my dear. It's too dreadful to contemplate.

LAURA. She could be the lunatic killer!

CHANDLER. *(matter-of-fact)* We've got more important things to worry about. I think we should layout a plan of action. Investigate, investigate, investigate.

LOUIS. Oui. Now is the time for all of us to be attentive, alert and vigilant. We must dot our "T's" and cross our "I's."

FATHER WHITE. Do you have a plan, Chandler? What do you suggest?

CHANDLER. Charity and me will tackle the wine cellar. Louis, you and Father White go over the upstairs with a fine-tooth comb.

LOUIS. We will leave no turn unstoned.

LAURA. What about me?

PETER. I'll take Laura with me. We'll check around outside.

LAURA. Is that wise?

PETER. Keep thinking about that twenty-five grand.

LAURA. Good point.

    (**PETER** *exits left.* **LAURA** *follows, turns.*)

    I'm so sorry about the wig.

CHARITY. So's my scalp.

    (**LAURA** *smiles, apologetic, exits.*)

CHANDLER. Charity, baby, here we are together once more. It's fate allover again.

CHARITY. Keep your mind on your work, Chandler.

(**CHARITY** *exits downstage right.* **CHANDLER** *follows.*)

CHANDLER. Sweet stuff, you've got me all wrong. What a dish! (*He exits.*)

LOUIS. False alibis, like blue cheese fondue, cannot stand the test of time.

FATHER WHITE. We've got work to do, Mr. Moto. Let's get to it.

(*He exits upstage center.* **LOUIS** *yells after him, exasperated.*)

LOUIS. I am not Mr. Moto! I am not Sam Spade! I am not Charlie Chan, Sherlock Holmes, or Hercule Poirot. I am Nancy Drew! (*flustered, to audience*) Make that Louis Croissant.

SONG – I AM LOUIS CROISSANT

(FIRST CHORUS)
I'M NOT MISTER MOTO
REMEMBER, IF YOU CAN.
THERE'S NO DEBATE, SET THE RECORD STRAIGHT.
MY NAME'S NOT CHARLIE CHAN.
DO NOT CALL ME SHERLOCK
FOR THAT NAME JUST ANNOYS.
I THINK YOU MIGHT TRY TO GET IT RIGHT.
I'M NOT THE HARDY BOYS.

LOUIS. (*cont.*) I AM NOT FROM NORWAY
OR FROM MEXICO.
I AM NOT A BELGIAN
LIKE HERCULE POIROT.

I'M NOT BULLDOG DRUMMOND
I AM NOT FU MANCHU.
SHOW SOME RESPECT, GET THE NAME CORRECT,
OR I SAY, "NUTS TO YOU."

(Second Chorus)

I'M NOT PERRY MASON.
THERE IS NO MASQUERADE.
THERE'S NO DEBATE, SET THE RECORD STRAIGHT,
MY NAME IS NOT SAM SPADE.

DON'T CALL ME DICK TRACY
BECAUSE I WON'T RESPOND.
I THINK YOU MIGHT TRY TO GET IT RIGHT.
MY NAME IS NOT JAMES BOND.

I AM NOT FROM DENMARK.
OR FROM TOYKO.
BUT I AM A FRENCHMAN
LIKE INSPECTOR CLOUSEAU.

SO PLEASE PAY ATTENTION
I'LL GIVE YOU ONE MORE CHANCE
THERE'S NO DEBATE, SET THE RECORD STRAIGHT,
I THINK YOU MIGHT TRY TO GET IT RIGHT,
SHOW SOME RESPECT, GET THE NAME CORRECT,
I AM MONSIEUR CROISSANT
VIVE LA FRANCE!

*(Song over, his wrath cooled, **LOUIS** exits Upstage Center in regal fashion, slow walk, head high. Pause. Lights flicker, gush of wind whips up. The door to secret passageway opens slightly.)*

MISS MAPLE'S VOICE. *(off downstage right)* I will not have fist-fights on the premises! *(**MISS MAPLE** enters.)* What's this about Charity Haze and Laura Carlyle fighting? *(looks)* Where is everyone?

(She steps into the room, notices the flickering lights.)

Oh, dear.

(Suddenly she senses something is not quite right in the room, starts to turn as the bookcase closes shut. She reacts to the sound.)

What was that?

(She looks about, sees nothing unusual.)

I'll read.

(Steps to the bookcase, selects a mystery novel.)

It'll quiet my nerves.

(She moves to the left center chair, sits, reads aloud.)

The Case of the Curious Caretaker…"I shall never forget the night I arrived at Skull Island…no one was there to greet me with the exception of Miss Midwinter the housekeeper, a woman of stern countenance and iron will…and I was terrified. Perhaps if the boatman had not been blind and mute some of my fears might have been lessened, but that was not to be. why was the bell in the abandoned tower ringing, I wondered? Did it foretell some dreaded happening…"

*(As she reads a **FIGURE** in gloves, long coat, hat, face covered by a scarf and dark glasses, enters from a secret passageway.)*

"…It wasn't the warmest of welcomes for a governess of sixteen…What would I encounter here, in this strange house of ancient rocks and dark emotions…"

(She realizes she's not alone, tenses. Sound of rain.)

Who's there? *(Panic seizes her.)* Who's there, I say?

*(She stands, faces the **INTRUDER** who darts back into the passageway and closes the bookcase.)*

Who are you? No, wait!

*(Crash of thunder. Shots ring out from downstage right. **MISS MAPLE** collapses in the chair with a dying groan. Sound of rain increases.)*

LAURA'S VOICE. Hurry!

PETER'S VOICE. I'm right behind you! *(They enter.)*

LAURA. Another moment and we'd be drenched.

PETER. If our killer's outside he's a fool as well as a madman.

*(**LAURA** tiptoes to **MISS MAPLE**.)*

LAURA. Sssssssh.

PETER. Hmmmmmmmm?

LAURA. How sweet. She's fallen asleep, like an innocent child.

PETER. Should we wake her?

LAURA. Let her sleep. She needs all the rest she can get.

(gets the afghan and tucks it around **MISS MAPLE***)*

She'll be fine.

*(***LAURA** *motions that he shouldn't make a sound, and the two of them tiptoe off upstage center. The lights dim leaving* **MISS MAPLE** *in a cold blue circle. Another figurine falls from the mantel.* **MISS MAPLE** *slumps. Another musical discord from the piano. Sound of rain up.)*

Scene Two

(AT RISE: Early morning. **MISS MAPLE** *remains slumped over.* **LOUIS** *and* **FATHER WHITE** *enter up center.)*

FATHER WHITE. We've searched everywhere. Not a sign of an intruder.

*(***CHARITY*** *and* ***CHANDLER*** *enter downstage right.)*

LOUIS. What did you two discover?

(All ignore the **HOSTESS.***)*

CHARITY. There's an embroidered bedsheet over the dead man.

LOUIS. Perhaps the killer, in a gesture of contrition, placed the embroidered bedsheet over the deceased.

FATHER WHITE. An embroidered bedsheet is a bit extravagant.

LOUIS. I suggest we consider the motive behind the placing of the embroidered bedsheet over the body of Rick Carlyle. It could possibly lead us to the killer's identity.

CHANDLER. You guys belong in a museum. The old doll had Rita toss the linen over the victim. Park it, Princess.

*(***CHARITY*** *sits on the sofa.* ***CHANDLER,*** *too.* ***FATHER WHITE*** *moves to doors, looks out)*

LOUIS. The mystery of the embroidered bedsheet is sol-ved. Louis Croissant has done it again.

CHANDLER. Louis, I don't think you could find yourself in the dark.

LOUIS. The dark is light enough when the brain is brilliant.

CHANDLER. Yuck.

*(***HAVERSHAM*** *enters downstage right.)*

HAVERSHAM. It ain't raining so much as before. *(She sniffles, sees* **MISS MAPLE.***)* What's the matter with her?

FATHER WHITE. Who?

HAVERSHAM. *(nods)* Miss Maple. *(All look.)*

FATHER WHITE. Bless me, I didn't see her sitting there.

CHARITY. She's awfully still.

LAURA. *(enters upstage center, overhearing)* She's exhausted.

HAVERSHAM. She don't look right to me.

(All look at the slumped over figure.)

LAURA. Napping, I tell you.

FATHER WHITE. I think we should wake her.

CHANDLER. Old people need sleep. Let her be.

LOUIS. She's as pale as a goat.

*(**PETER** enters upstage center, **LAURA** moves to bookcase.)*

PETER. Any luck?

CHANDLER. Naw.

FATHER WHITE. We've discovered exactly nothing.

*(**HAVERSHAM** sees broken figurine.)*

LAURA. I'm a widow and I want to know who made me one.

HAVERSHAM. *(picks up broken figurine)* It's another smashup.

LAURA. Another what?

HAVERSHAM. Another figurine fell off the mantel. It's broken like the first one.

LOUIS. This is most unusual. I tell you being a detective is no bed of noses.

HAVERSHAM. You don't get chinaware like this at a garage sale.

CHANDLER. Anybody got any ideas?

PETER. About what?

CHANDLER. About anything.

CHARITY. Why don't we get up a rubber of bridge?

AD LIBS. Splendid.

Why not?

Might relieve tension.

I'll be dummy.

Etc.

*(Enraged, **MISS MAPLE** flings aside the afghan, and stands.)*

MISS MAPLE. *Idiots! (All are startled.)* Didn't any one of you realize I was murdered!

OTHERS. Murdered?

LAURA. We thought you were asleep.

MISS MAPLE. Shots rang out. I was slumped over. A figurine fell from the mantel. You're a pack of incompetents. I arranged for Haversham to fire some blanks to test your reactions and you've failed miserably. Ladies and gentlemen, you disappoint me.

CHARITY. You were carrying on with the charade, right?

MISS MAPLE. That, Charity, is self-evident Since everything else has proven slightly absurd, I'm beginning to doubt that the gentleman in the cellar is truly deceased.

CHARITY. He's deceased.

CHANDLER. Take our word for it.

MISS MAPLE. I shall see for myself. You come with me, Haversham.

HAVERSHAM. Yes, ma'am. (**MISS MAPLE** *crosses down right, turns, denounces her guests with another –)*

MISS MAPLE. *Idiots!*

(She exits, **HAVERSHAM** *follows.)*

LAURA. *(calmly)* She's annoyed.

PETER. *(moves down center)* I hope this doesn't mean she'll give up the idea of the bookstores.

CHARITY. We better think up something to calm her down.

*(**RITA** enters upstage center with hat box.)*

RITA. You must be famished. There's some food that's sealed in it's container. No one could tamper with it. We might eat that.

LAURA. I am hungry.

RITA. There's plenty of fondue left.

LAURA. I'm on a diet.

RITA. I'll see what I can manage. *(moves downstage right)*

LOUIS. One moment, Miss Eyelesbarrow.

(**RITA** *turns.*)

RITA. You have something to say to me?

LOUIS. Do all of you remember when I suggested the killer was one of us?

RITA. Who could forget it? Are we back to that again?

AD LIBS. What?

You can't be serious?

That again.

LOUIS. Please let me explain. Why would the sweetheart of a heartless jockey take a job at Ravenswood Manor?

CHANDLER. Are you talking about the Kentucky Derby jockey?

LOUIS. I am.

CHANDLER. The jockey wasn't heartless. He was headless.

LOUIS. I believe Miss Eyelesbarrow is the jockey's sweetheart.

CHARITY. That's ridiculous.

LOUIS. I suggest that Rita Eyelesbarrow was also the sweetheart of Rick Carlyle, and when he wished to end the relationship, he was struck down as was the unfortunate jockey.

LAURA. You mean –

LOUIS. *(points)* There is the murderer. Fascinating and unscrupulous – Mabel Dupre!

(*All stare at* **RITA**. *She looks over her shoulder.*)

RITA. What's everyone staring at?

LOUIS. You are Mabel Dupre. You murdered Rick Carlyle. You are fascinating, unscrupulous and a killer.

LAURA. I don't want another mistake.

(**LOUIS** *takes newspaper clipping from pocket, hands it to* **LAURA**, *who moves downstage.*)

LOUIS. Here is a photograph from the newspaper showing the unhappy jockey and his mad sweetheart.

(**CHANDLER** *moves to* **LAURA**. *As do* **FATHER WHITE** *and* **PETER**.)

LOUIS. Note the positive resemblance.

(All look at clipping and then at **RITA**.*)*

The case is sol-ved.

PETER. Uh, Louie.

LOUIS. Yes?

PETER. The female in this picture is a black woman. Miss Eyelesbarrow is not a black woman.

CHARITY. *(to* **LOUIS***)* What a meatball.

LOUIS. Let me see the picture. *(He moves to others, takes clipping, studies it.)* Hmmmmmmm. *(to* **RITA***)* You are not the mad sweetheart.

RITA. You fool!

LOUIS. No violence, please. I bruise easily. (**LOUIS** *moves behind others for protection.)*

RITA. I'll get Miss Maple. She'll have a few choice words for you. You ought to be locked up. You're a menace. You, you – *hack. (She exits.)*

LOUIS. What? A hack? The unkindest cut of all. Insinuating that as a detective I have no talent or skill. I have been insulted but I will get over it. Time wounds all heels.

CHANDLER. *(moves behind* **CHARITY***)* I gotta hand it to you, Louis. You're one in a million. You couldn't guess right if you had the answers on a scoreboard.

FATHER WHITE. You do get carried away.

LOUIS. *(regally) When* all the hens cluck, who can hear the rooster?

(He walks upstage right, stands by console. **LAURA** *moves to left center chair, sits.)*

PETER. Question. Why was Rick the one to get it?

CHANDLER. *(vague)* Get what?

PETER. The dart in that chair.

(**LAURA** *gets up quickly, moves to the doors.)*

Oh, I am sorry, Laura. That was tactless.

LAURA. If only the dawn would get here.

(**MISS MAPLE** *enters.)*

MISS MAPLE. He's dead. Quite dead. There can be no mistake. *(over her shoulder)* What's this nonsense about Mr. Crossiant, Rita?

LOUIS. An error in judgment, dear hostess.

HAVERSHAM. You make a lot of those, don't you, Huey?

(**RITA** *enters.*)

RITA. I prefer to ignore Mr. Croissant's simple-minded and stupid deductions. I think I might be able to shed some light on this grisly affair.

CHANDLER. Speaking of grisly I don't suppose there's any chance of getting a hamburger?

(**MISS MAPLE** *moves to sofa and sits.*)

CHARITY. If you got something to say – say it.

RITA. Haversham.

CHANDLER. That ain't much.

CHARITY. What about her?

MISS MAPLE. Rita, what I told you about Haversham was in confidence.

RITA. I don't think we have any right to keep it a secret any longer.

LAURA. You mean about Haversham's police record?

MISS MAPLE. How did you know?

RITA. I told Mrs. Carlyle.

MISS MAPLE. Haversham isn't homicidal.

RITA. What about the "unpleasantness with the hatchet?"

LOUIS. Hatchet? Aha, we are back to the hat box.

RITA. Nothing of the sort.

PETER. Haversham? Hatchet? I recall the case. Made a splash on TV. Didn't she break into some safety-deposit boxes by chopping through the bank's outside wall?

MISS MAPLE. She made some such attempt.

HAVERSHAM. *(enters downstage right)* But I didn't get away with it, and I done my time. I'd appreciate it if you talked about me when I was in the room. It's only polite.

LOUIS. Murder and politeness seldom go together.

(thunder, the lights dim up and down.)

MISS MAPLE. Will this cursed storm never end?

(Positions at this point should be roughly as follows: **CHARITY** *and* **MISS MAPLE** *seated on the sofa.* **CHANDLER** *by the fireplace,* **RITA** *by the downstage end of sofa,* **HAVERSHAM** *downstage right.* **FATHER WHITE** *fry the left center chair,* **PETER** *left center,* **LOUIS** *by the console.* **LAURA** *by the doors.)*

CHARITY. *(speaks)* I think I can shed some light.

PETER. *(speaks)* Please do.

CHARITY. *(speaks)* We've reached the point where it's time for the classic "suspects in the drawing room" confrontation.

MISS MAPLE. *(speaks)* Whatever do you mean?

CHARITY. *(speaks)* You're all agreed that the murderer used the tape recording to layout his plan?

PETER. *(speaks)* Carlyle's demise was proof.

CHARITY. *(speaks)* Proof of nothing except that he was marked for death.

PETER. *(speaks)* What about you, Miss Haze? The recording accused you of murder.

CHARITY. *(speaks)* Murder only in the figurative sense. I'm good at killing-off characters in a book. Nothing more.

PETER. *(speaks)* The recording accused me of dishonor on the cricket field at Eton. Actually, I never attended Eton. I wanted people to think I had, but I never did. It was fabrication, nothing more. That's the dishonor.

FATHER WHITE. *(speaks)* I was accused of shaming my calling. I'm not really a Man-of-the-Cloth, though I've pretended to be. My shame is that I once acted as a religious advisor for a local production of *The Sound Of Music*.

ALL. *(speaking reactions)* Oh, no! How terrible! Etc.

CHARITY. *(speaks)* Well, what about the rest of us?

SONG – REVELATIONS

CHARITY.

LET'S PROVIDE SOME EXPLANATIONS.

CHANDLER. *(sings)*

THAT COULD CAUSE SOME COMPLICATIONS.

LAURA. *(sings)*

WE MUST GUARD OUR REPUTATIONS.

PETER. *(sings)*

I DENY ALL ALLEGATIONS.

RITA. *(sings)*

I DON'T LIKE THE IMPLICATIONS.

MISS MAPLE. *(sings)*

I SUSPECT SOME FABRICATIONS.

LOUIS. *(sings)*

LET'S REVEAL OUR MOTIVATIONS.

FATHER WHITE. *(sings)*

IT IS TIME FOR REVELATIONS.

(speaks)

Not in the Biblical sense, of course. But revelations, none-the-less.

CHARITY. *(speaks)* Yeah, it's Confession Time. What about you, Rita? Tell us all about your hat box.

RITA. *(sings)*

I'VE A SECRET HIDDEN IN THE HAT BOX

BUT NOT THE KIND OF SECRET YOU SUSPECT.

IT IS TRUE A HEAD IS IN THE HAT BOX,

BUT IT'S A HEAD OF CABBAGE FOR "EFFECT."

ALL. *(spoken)* Cabbage!

LOUIS. *(spoken)* A head of cabbage is food for thought.

CHARITY. *(spoken)* How about you, Louie? What about the night in Shanghai?

LOUIS. *(sings)*

"NIGHT IN SHANGHAI" IS A MYST'RY NOVEL.

A BOOK I WROTE TO CRITICAL SUCCESS.

I STOLE THE PLOT AND TITLE FROM ANOTHER

AND HAD IT PUBLISHED FIRST, I DO CONFESS.

ALL. *(spoken)* Plagiarism!

LOUIS. *(spoken)* Yes, "Night in Shanghai" does not refer to a holiday in the Orient.

CHARITY. *(spoken)* What about you, Mrs. Carlyle? What does "Tulip" signify?

LAURA. *(sings)*
TULIP WAS A CHARMING LITTLE PUPPY
THE KIND OF DOG YOU SIMPLY CAN'T IGNORE.
RICK AND I PERFORMED AN INDISCRETION
ABDUCTING LITTLE TULIP FROM THE STORE.

ALL. *(spoken)* Dognappers!

LAURA. *(speaks)* We wanted to buy him, but the pet store owner refused. We changed Tulip's name to Napoleon so no one would know. How would it look in the society pages?

CHARITY. *(speaks)* It's your turn, Marlowe. The recording said you were guilty of a foul crime.

CHANDLER. *(speaks)* Being a sitting duck on Turkey Island is "fowl" enough.

ALL. *(chiding)* Marlowe!

CHANDLER. *(sings)*
LONG BEFORE I WROTE DETECTIVE STORIES
I WROTE WITH A STYLE MORE ANALYTIC.
MAKING THIS CONFESSION ISN'T EASY.
BUT I WAS ONCE A LITERARY CRITIC!

ALL. *(spoken)* A critic!

MISS MAPLE. *(speaks)* That *is* foul.

CHARITY. Only one thing matters. Who killed Carlyle? *(sits)*

CHANDLER. We don't know if the tape recording and the murderer are one and the same. *(Moves to desk. All eyes are following him.)* What we have to decide is who had the motive and the opportunity to knock off Carlyle. *(picks up pad and pencil)* The killer had to know the house.

MISS MAPLE. Could it have been the man in the dark glasses and scarf? *(long pause)*

CHANDLER. Who?

MISS MAPLE. A moment before I was shot. He was in this room. Didn't I tell you? (*All shake their heads.*) It must have slipped my mind. Do you think it was someone playing another little joke, enjoying the charade?

CHANDLER. I'll deal with that later. Let me go on with my deducing. Remember those key words – "motive"- "opportunity."

(*As he starts to cross right, his foot some how manages to get stuck in the wastebasket and he has trouble getting it out. All watch.*)

CHARITY. Chandler, for goodness sake.

(*Telephone rings.*)

MISS MAPLE. What's that?

HAVERSHAM. It's a telephone.

MISS MAPLE. There is no telephone on Turkey Island.

RITA. (*moves stage right*) It's coming from over here.

LAURA. (*points*) The desk.

FATHER WHITE. There's no phone on the desk.

CHANDLER. (*still busy with wastebasket, sits at desk*) Try the drawer.

(**RITA** *opens one drawer, then another, phone continues to ring. She finds the phone, takes it out. All tense.*)

HAVERSHAM. Answer it.

(*Leery,* **RITA** *picks up the receiver.*)

RITA. Ravenswood Manor.

LOUIS. Who is the caller?

(**RITA** *frowns, listens a moment longer, puts down receiver, replaces it in the drawer.*)

MISS MAPLE. What did they say?

RITA. I'd rather not repeat what I heard. Anyway, it was mostly heavy breathing.

CHANDLER. (*ignores interruption*) Who had "motive" and who had "opportunity."

(*Phone rings again. All tense.*)

Let me handle it - in the detective game you're either a firecracker or a fizzle. *(He stands, foot still in the wastebasket opens drawer, takes out phone, lifts receiver.)* This is Chandler Marlowe speaking, you pinhead. I have ways of tracing phone calls and when I find out who you are I'm going to rearrange your face. You're going to be breathing through your navel…your chin's going to be on the top of your head.

(CHANDLER, unlike RITA, has pulled the phone all the way out from the drawer so everyone can clearly see the cord is severed. CHANDLER continues on.)

Is that so…you think you're man enough…you just remember my name, buster…Chandler Marlowe.

(He sees everyone glaring at him. He notices the severed cord, grins sheepishly, replaces the phone.)

MISS MAPLE. Mr. Marlowe, would you mind explaining?

CHANDLER. Uh, well, ha, ha. Part of the charade. You wanted us to keep it up, didn't you?

CHARITY. But the telephone rang.

CHANDLER. I've got a relay buzzer in my pocket.

(Sticks his hand in pocket, pretends to trigger some buzzer mechanism. Phone rings.)

HAVERSHAM. Shall I answer it?

MISS MAPLE. Do shut up, you silly girl.

(Insulted, HAVERSHAM exits downstage right.)

RITA. Better tell it all, Chandler.

MISS MAPLE. Rita, what do you have to do with this?

RITA. I'm Chandler's secretary.

FATHER WHITE. You?

RITA. When Miss Maple advertised for a social secretary, Chandler had me apply.

CHANDLER. I already had my invitation, So I thought it was a great opportunity for some laughs. I kept needling Louis about the Headless Horseman until I had him thinking it was Rita who did the jockey in. Louis is easy to fool.

MISS MAPLE. *(critical)* I know.

LAURA. Father White knows this house inside and out. *(points to bookcase)* I saw him coming out of that wall.

CHANDLER. He's a bookworm, eh? Ha, ha.

LAURA. There's a secret passageway back there.

FATHER WHITE. What if there is?

CHANDLER. Secret passageway? That's what I like to hear. Now we're getting somewhere.

RITA. It's not a secret passageway. The original owner had a flair for eccentric architecture. It leads up from the wine cellar.

MISS MAPLE. Oh, is that where the other door is?

PETER. Didn't you know?

MISS MAPLE. This isn't my home. I merely rented it for a few weeks for the purpose of this weekend house party. That's the real secret of Ravenswood Manor.

(sound of helicopter)

CHANDLER. Listen!

RITA. The helicopter.

MISS MAPLE. Maybe this time it IS the police.

(All rush to doors.)

LAURA. Can you see it?

LOUIS. It's too dark.

MISS MAPLE. Is it at the dock or over the house?

CHANDLER. I think it's on the north side of the island.

CHARITY. We could signal with a flare.

CHANDLER. Through the kitchen. Out that way.

(All rush downstage right. During this distraction, **CHARITY** *slips out the doors.* **RITA** *remains by the desk.* **CHANDLER** *is still fighting the wastebasket, stomping about.)*

FATHER WHITE. Signaling the helicopter may be our last chance.

MISS MAPLE. We must get its attention.

(Sound of helicopter fades. Bookcase slowly swings open.)

RITA. Wait! Look!

(Others stop and turn at **RITA***'s words. All stare at book-case. A moment passes and the* **INDIVIDUAL** *Miss Maple saw previously, still dressed in hat, glasses, gloves, long coat, enters.)*

MISS MAPLE. It's him. The man I was telling you about!

(There is a moment of dramatic suspense as the man in the passageway takes off the hat, the scarf the glasses.)

FATHER WHITE. Good Lord – Rick Carlyle!

MISS MAPLE. It's not possible. You're dead.

CHANDLER. *He was dead.*

RICK. *(moves stage center)* I, too, thought of a little joke that would be amusing. Instead of one Rick Carlyle there would be two.

LOUIS. Two?

LAURA. Rick's twin brother. He's the one down in the wine cellar.

RICK. I was going to confuse everyone, be in two places at the same time. Only someone got to me first and finished me off.

CHANDLER. You mean finished your brother off, don't you?

RICK. The murderer didn't know he had made a mistake, so I decided to stay out of sight and learn what I could.

CHANDLER. *(still struggling with the wastebasket)* What did you learn?

RICK. Nothing.

PETER. *(His voice and manner are slightly different.)* I'll take it from here.

LOUIS. *(points)* You – You are the murderer.

PETER. Wrong again.

LOUIS. Rats.

MISS MAPLE. You'll take what from here?

PETER. *(moves to center)* The investigation. I saw Carlyle talking with his brother in town. Carlyle's twin was a con artist. If he was coming here, he had plans to rob. Flimsey owes me a favor or two, so taking his place was no problem.

RICK. My brother did seem to agree rather quickly to my plan. I should have suspected.

PETER. The pickings would be good. Some jewels, some wallets. Who knows what else?

CHARITY. If you're not Peter Flimsey, who are you? *(He takes out an I.D. wallet displays badge.)*

PETER. Pharaoh Link.

CHANDLER. Crack investigator on the 'Frisco force.

PETER. *(corrects)* That's San Francisco. Can't you get your foot out of that wastebasket?

CHANDLER. I'm trying.

> *(HAVERSHAM enters downstage right. CHANDLER pulls out his foot PETER moves Left. MISS MAPLE sits on sofa. HAVERSHAM edges up to fireplace.)*

MISS MAPLE. It was all a charming and delightful exercise.

> *(HAVERSHAM moves upstage center.)*

RITA. Haven't you forgotten something?

MISS MAPLE. I don't think so.

RITA. Something *important*.

MISS MAPLE. Like what?

RITA. *Who killed the crook in the wine cellar!!!*

> *(HAVERSHAM speaks out her voice strong, powerful, threatening.)*

HAVERSHAM. Let me answer that!

> *(Fast, she pulls off her glasses, fluffs out her hair and strips off the too-large dress to reveal a shapely figure dressed in the latest chic fashion. She's a knockout.)*

PETER. Who are you, Miss?

RICK. *Mabel!*

LAURA. Mabel? Oh, Rick. *(***LAURA*** goes to ***RICK****'s arms.)*

LOUIS. *(points to ***HAVERSHAM***)* You – you are the murderer.

CHARITY. If you say that one more time, I'll murder you.

*(***MABEL*** lifts the hem of her short skirt. There's a small pistol secure in the top of her hose. She pulls it out, aims.)*

HAVERSHAM. This time Louie rings the bell. I am the murderer.

LOUIS. Louis Croissant has done it again! Another case sol-ved.

HAVERSHAM. *(to ***RICK***)* I killed the wrong man. I won't make that mistake a second time.

MISS MAPLE. Where is the real Haversham?

HAVERSHAM. Probably in Canada by now. I gave her two hundred dollars to take her place.

MISS MAPLE. I won't be able to give a good report to the parole people.

HAVERSHAM. *(indicates ***RICK***)* You made a fool of me. No one walks out on Mabel Dupre.

LAURA. Rick, is she going to shoot?

RICK. Not until she sings.

*(She sings. NOTE: As ***MABEL*** sings she moves about the room, aiming her gun from one character to another. They react by cowering, ducking, stepping aside, etc.)*

SONG – FEMME FATALE

HAVERSHAM/MABEL DUPRE.

> *(verse)*
> WHEN I WAS GROWING UP
> I DIDN'T PLAY WITH DOLLS.
> MY PARENTS THOUGHT THAT IT WAS QUAINT.
> LIKE WASHINGTON I MUCH PREFERRED A HATCHET
> AND LIZZIE BORDEN WAS MY PATRON SAINT.

> *(first refrain)*
> THERE ARE GUYS WHO LIKE TO HEAR A STEPHEN
>   SONDHEIM SCORE.
> THERE ARE GUYS WHO LIKE TO HEAR THE SONGS FROM
>   "PINAFORE."

BUT WITH ME, THEY'RE GONNA HEAR DEATH KNOCKING AT
    THE DOOR
I'M A FEMME FATALE.
FROM A SIMPLE KISS THERE ARE SOME GUYS WHO MIGHT
    ASSUME
THAT THE KISS WILL LEAD TO SOMETHING KNOWN AS
    "BRIDE AND GROOM."
BUT A KISS FROM ME JUST MEANS I'M GONNA SEAL HIS
    DOOM.
I'M A FEMME FATALE.

BE ON GUARD
EVRY HE-MALE.
THERE'S NOTHING DEADLIER
THAN THIS FEMALE.

THERE ARE GIRLS WHO DRESS UP WITH A FASHION
    MODEL'S SKILL
THERE ARE GIRLS WHO DRESS IN MINK TO STOP A WINTRY
    CHILL
BUT NO MATTER WHAT I WEAR, I'M ALWAYS "DRESSED TO
    KILL"
I'M A FEMME FATALE.

(second chorus)
THERE ARE GUYS WHO TAKE ME JOGGING IN THE
    COUNTRYSIDE
THERE ARE GUYS WHO LIKE TO TAKE ME SWIMMING WITH
    THE TIDE.
BUT WITH ME, I ALWAYS TAKE THE FELLA FOR A RIDE.
I'M A FEMME FATALE.

THERE ARE GIRLS WHO LIKE TO SEE A FELLA NEATLY
    DRESSED
THERE ARE GIRLS WHO LIKE TO SEE A FELLA'S MANLY
    CHEST
BUT I LIKE TO SEE A GUY AT HIS ETERNAL REST.
I'M A FEMME FATALE.

BE ON GUARD
IT'S FOR CERTAIN
THAT I WILL RING DOWN
YOUR FINAL CURTAIN.

THERE ARE GIRLS WHO LIKE A GUY TO MERELY BE A CHUM.
THERE ARE GIRLS WHO LIKE TO HOLD A GUY BENEATH
   THEIR THUMB
BUT I LIKE A GUY WHEN HE IS "IN MEMORIAM."
I'M A FEMME FATALE.

JUST BRING ON SOME MORE MALES
AND THEY'LL BE DEAD-AS-DOORNAILS
WHEN THEY MEET UP WITH A FEMME FATALE.

RICK. You'll never get away with it, Mabel!

HAVERSHAM. *(aims at* **RICK***)* Oh, no? Watch!

(General pandemonium as **CHARITY** *leaps in from Upstage Center, gives the firing wrist a karate chop. The* **GUN FIRES** *into the carpet* **CHARITY** *jumps behind* **MABEL** *and gets her in a backarm lock.)*

CHANDLER. What a woman!

MISS MAPLE. You're a wonder.

PETER. The police helicopter is flying around to see if I need assistance. It's going to have an unexpected passenger. I'm taking you in.

(He moves to **MABEL***, puts on a pair of cuffs.)*

MISS MAPLE. Look, it's dawn.

(All look to the doors. If possible, a bright lighting effect is brought in from outside to simulate blazing dawn.)

FATHER WHITE. And the storm has passed. That means a boat from the mainland will be here soon.

PETER. *(pushing her out)* Mabel, you've got a date with a jury.

HAVERSHAM. *(head high)* I won't have anything to worry about. Not if there are twelve men on that jury.

LOUIS. Cherchez la femme.

ALL. *(to audience)* That's French, you know.

*(***PETER** *and* **MABEL** *exit.)*

LAURA. I don't want to stay in this place another minute.

FATHER WHITE. Let's get our luggage and let's get out of here.

(**CHANDLER, FATHER WHITE, LOUIS, RICK** *and* **LAURA** *move upstage center.*)

CHARITY. I didn't bring any luggage. Maybe I can hitch a ride with Pharaoh Link. He's my kind of man. (**CHARITY** *exits left.*)

CHANDLER. Pharaoh Link? Hey, Charity, remember me? Jungle love. How do you like that? I should know better than to trust a dame I met while I was in a gorilla suit.

(He shakes his head like the cynical cuss he is, exits upstage center after the others.)

MISS MAPLE. Rita, I said we'd have a marvelous weekend. It didn't quite turn out the way I planned. Still, you must admit Miss Maple delivers what Miss Maple promises. Murder –

RITA. Mystery –

MISS MAPLE. Mayhem.

(They start to sing a reprise of THE BUTLER DID IT – and as they do, **ENTIRE CAST** *moves onstage [including* **STAFF**] *and joins in a lively finale.)*

SONG – THE BUTLER DID IT

(ALL OR DIVIDED BY GROUPS .)
WE THOUGHT THE BUTLER DID IT.
WE THOUGHT THE BUTLER DID IT.
YES, WE THOUGHT HE CAUSED THIS MURDEROUS AFFAIR.
WE THOUGHT THE BUTLER DID IT.
WE THOUGHT THE BUTLER DID IT.
ALTHOUGH WE HAVEN'T SEEN A BUTLER ANYWHERE.

IT MIGHT HAVE BEEN THE BUTLER,
IT MIGHT HAVE BEEN THE BUTLER.
YES, HE COULD HAVE CAUSED THIS FRIGHTFUL FOLDEROL.
IT MIGHT HAVE BEEN THE BUTLER,
IT MIGHT HAVE BEEN THE BUTLER.
THOUGH WE HAVEN'T SEEN A BUTLER HERE AT ALL.

EV'RY GUEST WHO WAS INVITED
WAS SUSPICIOUS AS COULD BE.

THOUGH IT'S AWFUL TO DISCUSS
STILL THE FRAUD WAS ONE OF US
AND I DEFINITELY KNEW IT WASN'T ME.

WE THOUGHT THE BUTLER DID IT.
WE THOUGHT THE BUTLER DID IT.
THOUGH IT SOUNDS, WE KNOW, LIKE SUCH AN OLD
    CLICHE.
WE THOUGHT IT WAS THE BUTLER,
IT ALWAYS IS THE BUTLER
THOUGH WE HAVEN'T SEEN A BUTLER HERE TODAY.

WE THOUGHT IT WAS THE BUTLER.
IT ALWAYS IS THE BUTLER
ON THAT POINT WE ALL AGREE.
WE KNEW WITH OUT
A SHADOW OF A DOUBT
THAT IT DEFINITELY,
POSITIVELY,
ABSOLUTELY
WASN'T ME!

The End

PRODUCTION NOTES

STAGE PROPERTIES

Fireplace with mantel, three figurines, portrait, console, bookcase with books (secret passageway), desk with paper and pencil, wastebasket, telephone (in drawer). Additional stage dressing (rugs, lamps, small tables, chairs, etc.) – as desired.

HAND AND PERSONAL PROPERTIES

ACT ONE: Hat box (**RITA**), eyeglasses (**MISS MAPLE**), umbrella (**FATHER WHITE**), toy dog (**RICK**), gun (**CHANDLER**), tray with plate of biscuits and glasses of sherry (**HAVERSHAM**), flashlight (**FATHER WHITE**), magnifying glass (**PETER**).

ACT TWO: Afghan (**RITA**), newspaper clipping (**LOUIS**), I.D. wallet with badge (**PETER**), gun (**HAVERSHAM**), handcuffs (**PETER**).

SOUND EFFECTS

Motorboat. gunshot, helicopter, storm effects, telephone. All required sound effects available through Baker's Plays. For more information, please consult the Baker's Plays website, BakersPlays.com.

COSTUMES

Mentioned here are only those costumes necessary to plot large maid's dress, eyeglasses (**HAVERSHAM**), raincoat, hat (**CHANDLER**), raincoat, hat (**LOUIS**), goggles, helmet, raincoat (**CHARITY**). Some nice visual touches can be made in costuming, if desired. For example, **RICK** and **LAURA** might arrive in evening clothes, **CHARITY** might arrive in a jumpsuit, etc.

MISCELLANEOUS

1. GENERAL STYLE: Play up the spoof aspects as much as possible. Exaggerate the costuming, make the set "amusingly spooky," let the acting lean to the overdone.
2. DANCE: Several of the musical numbers can accommodate some choreography. Be inventive. The *Cherchez La Femme* number, with the male detectives going into "A Chorus Line"/Rockettes-style dance finale, is a big audience pleaser. Have the male detectives roll up their trousers at one point.

3. DEATH SCENE: When **RICK** (twin brother) dies, play it up for all it's worth. Victim should stammer, struggle and thrash about. The more outrageous the better.

4. STAGE LIGHTING: Not too bright. Gothic mysteries, even spoofs, need shadows. Having the dawn flash on as if someone pulled a light switch is a comic touch that gets another big laugh.

5. TRANSFORMATION OF HAVERSHAM INTO MABEL DUPRE: When **HAVERSHAM** gets out of her baggy dress, glasses, hair style, she should look dazzling. Nice touch is to have the stage arch trimmed with colored lights. As soon as **MABEL** stands defiantly as her true personality, the lights flash on in "Hello, Dolly" fashion. Same bit can be used in Act I when **CHARITY** takes off her helmet and her gorgeous hair is revealed.

6. THE STAFF: If staff is used, improvise some business – for example, as the madness plays along, have a **MAID** enter from downstage right with some linen and exit upstage center. **GARDNER**, in a raincoat, can enter and place a bouquet of flowers; **CHAUFFEUR** can appear with a spare tire, etc. The **STAFF** pays absolutely no attention to whatever is taking place onstage. **STAFF** is detached, aloof and unruffled.

AUTHOR'S NOTES

In the program don't forget to list the fictitious roles of **MABEL DUPRE** and **PHAROAH LINK**, as well as the fictitious actors.. This way the audience assumes two "new" characters are always about to appear and shed some light on the mystery. The **RADIO VOICE** must come across loud and clear. In the final scene be careful not to rush the dialog because there's much that the audience has to digest and speed will only cut down on the laughs and minimize the overall effect. Pauses and reactions are most important here. Remember that characters are always entering and exiting through the double or French doors, so make certain they are closed after a character has entered or left. A door that stands open on stage, especially in a thriller script, always diverts attention. **MABEL**'s pistol shot can come from offstage, actress doesn't have to actually fire the prop.

www.ingramcontent.com/pod-product-compliance
Lightning Source LLC
Chambersburg PA
CBHW061040050726
47592CB00004B/1525